AMANDA FARLEY 2.75

POLITICAL REALITIES
Edited on behalf of the
by Bernard Crick

ADELA.   ARY

PLEA   JRN BY

LONGMAN GROUP LIMITED
Longman House
Burnt Mill, Harlow, Essex, UK

First published 1982
ISBN 0 582 35302 5 (cased)
ISBN 0 582 35303 3 (paper)

Set in TR 10/12 VIP

Printed in Hong Kong by
Wilture Enterprises (International) Ltd

Acknowledgements
We are indebted to the following for permission to reproduce copyright
material:
Anthony Wedgwood Benn for an extract from a letter to constituents, January
1975.

Contents

Political Realities: the Nature of the Series

A great need is felt for short books which can supplement or even replace textbooks and which can deal in an objective but realistic way with problems that arouse political controversy. The series aims to break from a purely descriptive and institutional approach to one that will show how and why there are different interpretations both of how things work and how they ought to work. Too often in the past 'British Constitution' has been taught quite apart from any knowledge of the actual political conflicts which institutions strive to contain. So the Politics Association continues to sponsor this now well-established series because it believes that a specifically civic education is an essential part of any liberal or general education, but that respect for political rules and an active citizenship can only be encouraged by helping pupils, students and young voters to discover what are the main objects of political controversy, the varying views about the nature of the constitution – themselves often highly political, and what are the most widely canvassed alternative policies in their society. From such a realistic appreciation of differences and conflicts reasoning can then follow about the common processes of containing or resolving them peacefully.

The specific topics chosen are based on an analysis of the main elements in existing A level syllabuses, and the manner in which they are treated is based on the conviction of the editors that almost every examination board has been moving, slowly but surely, away from a concentration on constitutional rules and towards the more difficult but important concept of a realistic political education or the enhancement of political literacy.

This approach has, of course, been common enough in the universities for many years. Quite apart from its civic importance, the teaching of politics in schools has tended to lag behind university practice and expectations. So the editors have aimed to draw on the most up-to-date academic knowledge, the books being written by a wide spectrum of authors, but all aware of the need to combine accurate scholarship with lucid presentation.

The Politics Association and the editors are conscious of the great importance of other levels of education, and have been actively pursuing studies and projects of curriculum development in several directions. But A level and new developments in sixth-form courses are recognised as being important precisely because of the great overlap here between teaching in secondary school and further education colleges, whether specifically for examinations or not; indeed most of the books will be equally useful for general studies, just as several are also widely used by first year students in universities and polytechnics.

Bernard Crick
Derek Heater

Foreword

In the late twentieth century, a growing number of the issues which concern our daily lives have moved beyond the control of national governments. Rapidly diminishing world supplies of raw materials, energy and food and developments in nuclear science threaten the safety of the world. Complex industrial processes require economic and international cooperative action, while industrial pollution may spread to the rivers and beaches of an entire continent. Terrorism too has become internationalised, as disaffected groups try to draw world-wide attention to their grievances.

Only the continental-wide 'superpowers', like the United States and the Soviet Union, with vast land and mineral resources behind them, can still think in terms of solving their major problems at national level. For smaller powers, including the medium-sized nation states of Western Europe, many decisions, over defence and security, for example, have to be taken within wider alliances. In the economic field too, national governments cannot take decisions without first consulting overseas partners or creditors, whose interests may also be affected.

Within industrialised and technologically advanced societies, like those of Western Europe, increasing prosperity and rising educational standards have revolutionised life-styles over the past thirty years. People have begun to demand more from society. They have become aware of their interests as consumers of the goods and services society has to offer, and of the environmental risks involved in their production. As industrial workers, they may feel alienated from a society in which the ownership and control of industry still seem to be too far removed from the producers. Ordinary citizens are for the first time ready and able to demand more effective action from government in areas where their interests are affected. They expect governments to act more openly, so that they may see what is being done on their behalf. Industrial and technological societies need to be centralised for efficiency, but they also require some devolution of power from the centre, to allow for citizen involvement.

In the rapidly changing social climate of Western Europe, we have needed to re-examine the purpose of government and administration, and to look more critically at the political structures which we have inherited. We have needed to consider the level of government which is most appropriate to the kind of tasks it has to perform and to look for the type of organisation which will give ordinary people both a sense of belonging and an opportunity to participate. Traditional government processes at the level of the nation state are no longer necessarily the most efficient, and politics in Western Europe over the past thirty years has been preoccupied with attempts to set up more manageable and effective political units, both within the state, at regional, neighbourhood and factory level, and beyond it, at the continental level. A 'multi-tiered' approach to government and to decision-making has begun to take shape.

Political action must be effective and capable of achieving its intended results. A world level of government, for example, is at present too distant a prospect for practical consideration. But in Western Europe, a political structure at supranational level has already come into being. The European Economic Community, set up by the Treaty of Rome in 1958, was an attempt to maintain peace in Europe and to achieve prosperity through cooperation. At present it is predominantly an economic grouping, but it also contains some shared institutions and joint decision-making in limited, carefully defined areas. It is partly due to the achievements of the Economic Community that within forty years of the ending of the Second World War, we take it for granted that armed combat between the protagonists of that war, now partners within the Community, would be unthinkable. During those years the countries of Western Europe recovered fully from the devastations of war, became prosperous and were able to hold their own in the post-war world of advancing technology and growing superpowers.

It is now over twenty years since the signing of the Treaty of Rome, and since that time profound changes have taken place in the political, social and, above all, the economic realities of Europe. The industrialised nation states of Western Europe are now precariously dependent upon scarce imported raw materials, energy and minerals.

They are individually too small and too densely populated to take full advantage of the scale of modern industrial and technological developments. They face competition from the United States and Japan, and from the rapidly developing industrialised nations of the Third World. Europe's own industries have moved beyond national frontiers and are dominated by a handful of multinational companies. Governments themselves are increasingly concerned in the management of declining industries. Supranational planning, decision-making and action have become even more necessary than they were when the excesses of National Socialism first provided the impetus for European integration to get under way. Yet the nation states at the beginning of the 1980s still remain Europe's most effective and powerful political reality.

Government at the level of a continental grouping could be an appropriate level at which to approach at least some of the problems of the modern world. Yet many Europeans are not convinced that European joint action, beyond that needed for the functioning of the existing Customs Union and Common Market is either necessary or desirable, nor that there are political functions which will give better results because they are performed at Community rather than at any other level of government. The Economic Community itself still has to demonstrate that it has the potential to develop further political functions as the need for them becomes accepted by the member states.

This book is a brief attempt to increase understanding of the nature of the existing European Community, its historical and political origins, and, in particular, the workings of its complex institutions and processes. It attempts to assess the relevance of the Community to the citizens who live within it, its standing in the world, its chances of survival through adaptation to changing circumstances and of developing into a wider political grouping, should that role be a desirable one for such a Community to play in Europe's future.

The European Community of the 1980s grew out of the political and economic circumstances and was shaped by the personalities of post-Second World War Europe. It began as a Customs Union and a Common Market. In the Treaty of Rome it was described as an Economic Community and at the beginning of the 1980s it is still dominated by concern for economic growth and for the commercial market.

One of the most striking aspects of post-war international relations was the way in which diplomatic and strategic issues of foreign policy gave way increasingly to commercial and financial affairs. Economic integration was not the only approach to European unification after the Second World War, but it was a reflection of the political realities of the second half of the twentieth century, that the economic aspects of life eventually brought Europeans together, despite the fact that it was a vision of political integration which had inspired European idealists throughout centuries of European history.

scale: 0   500   1000 km

first members (1958)

new members (1973)

new member (1981)

candidate countries

The European Economic Community: member states and candidate countries

1 From Federalist Idealism to Common Market

A United States of Europe

The idea of European unification was a persistent theme in European political thought. It was kept alive by scholars who remembered that Europeans shared a common inheritance of Greek philosophy and Christian religious beliefs; but who also knew that for four centuries much of the Europe we know today had been united within the strong legal and political framework of the Roman Empire.

As the centuries passed and Europeans continued to fight each other, first over religious differences, then over dynastic and colonial rivalries, from time to time idealistic plans would resurface for cooperation, rather than conflict, between the states of Europe. Most were inspired by Christian beliefs, like the Duc de Sully's 'Grand Design' for a 'most Christian Council' of Europe, backed by a European peace-keeping army, which he proposed during the reign of Henri IV of France; or the Catholic Abbé de Saint Pierre's proposal in 1712 for a European senate, backed by an alliance between European rulers, based on an agreement to take decisions by majority vote.

During the years when the nation states were at their most powerful, exchanges of ideas continued across national frontiers. Throughout Europe too there were basic similarities in social structure. Each dynastic monarch ruled over a predominantly agricultural community, a landed gentry and a powerful church. In the first half of the eighteenth century, young men from the wealthy and educated classes of each country made the 'Grand Tour', met their contemporaries and exchanged ideas in French, the common language of the educated classes. In the early nineteenth century Napoleon's revolutionary schemes for uniting Europe by force under French domination were countered by a fierce national self-assertiveness. Industrialisation and urban life contributed to the development of the Socialist political movement in nineteenth-century Europe and some socialist theorists, notably Proudhon, argued that a federation of European nations was necessary to guarantee the interests of the smaller countries and their workers. But international socialism took a different path and most European socialists continued to work within national movements and to pursue national objectives. National ambition and self-interest remained the predominant political forces in Europe throughout the century and it was finally the disasters of the two world wars, in the first half of the twentieth century, both fought primarily for national advantages, which led to the serious study of European integration by peaceful methods, as a possible political alternative to the independent and aggressive nation state.

Federalism and functional cooperation

Political integration, the peaceful creation of a larger political unit out of several previously separate ones, each of which voluntarily gives up some powers to a central authority and renounces the use of force towards the other participants,[1] remained an idealists' pipe-dream until the 1920s, when a Pan-European movement, led by Richard Coudenhove-Kalergi, a count of the old Holy Roman Empire, at last won support from two practising European statesmen. Both Aristide Briand, the French Foreign Minister from 1925–32 and Gustav Stresemann, German Foreign Minister from 1923–29, saw in the idea of a federal United States of Europe the possibility of preventing a return to war.

In the years between the two world wars a number of international agencies were founded to carry out some of the technical, politically neutral functions which governments were expected to perform in modern states; agencies for Posts and Telegraphs, Shipping and Aircraft, Health and Labour were established. Their supporters believed not only that international collaboration over such functions was effective but that it would lead to closer political cooperation in other fields. But those who supported European integration, federalist and functionalist alike, remained outside the mainstream of political thought and were swept aside by the political forces which emerged in Europe in the years following the Great Depression. The military tyrannies of the Fascists and the Nazis were closely identified with nationalism. The failure of Europe's old-established nation states to maintain their independence or to defend the lives of their citizens against aggression led to bitter disillusionment. Only the Soviet Union and Great Britain were still predisposed, psychologically at least, by their experiences in the Second World War, to national autonomy.

Federalism in post-war Europe

In the prison camps and among the resistance movements of Nazi-dominated Europe, 'the underground Europe of the maquis and the false papers', as Albert Camus, the novelist and thinker, then editing an underground newspaper in occupied France, referred to it, the idea of a European Federation had surfaced once again. 'Libérer et fédérer' was one of the slogans of the French resistance movement, but the federalist idea seemed to grow simultaneously, not only in France, but in the German, Italian, Dutch, Czech, Yugoslav and Polish underground movements too.

Altiero Spinelli, later to become a Commissioner of the European Economic Community in Brussels, has described[2] how in 1940 a group of men imprisoned by Mussolini on an island off the Italian coast, planned for a post-war Europe in which a European authority would take over the conduct of foreign policy, defence and economic affairs, the areas where national governments were considered to have failed so disastrously before the war. In July 1944, resistance leaders from all over Europe met in Geneva. They condemned the part played by nationalism in the rise of fascism and pledged themselves to the creation of a European Federal Union, a united Europe that would prevent the outbreak of war in future, with a government directly responsible to the people of the member states, an army and a supreme court. The first European Federalist Congress met in Paris in March 1945 and a Europe-wide movement was founded 'to promote the federal organisation of the European peoples'.

Convinced federalists like the Swiss writer Denis de Rougemont and the Dutchman Henry Brugmans believed that international cooperation would not be enough. They would have to create joint institutions to exercise some of the powers held by national governments and they called for the formation of a European constituent assembly. At about the same time the French economist and administrator, Jean Monnet, influenced by the ideas of the pre-war functionalists, was arguing that European unity could be achieved through the creation of specialised administrative bodies at European level, which, by carrying out their specific functions successfully, would be able to attract political authority to themselves and away from national governments. A third approach to the unification of Europe was a consequence of Winston Churchill's early recognition that in post-war Europe some joint action in the conduct of affairs would be needed.

Churchill and the Council of Europe

In a famous speech which he made in Zurich in September 1946 Churchill, who had already during the war proposed a post-war European nation of at least ten states, including the former great powers, governed by a joint Council and backed by a European High Court and with its own armed forces, now called for the construction of 'a kind of United States of Europe'.

A United Europe Committee under his Chairmanship was formed in London, with Léon Blum, the leader of the French Socialist Party, Alcide de Gasperi, the Italian Prime Minister and leader of the Italian Christian Democratic Party, and the Belgian Socialist Foreign Minister, Paul-Henri Spaak, among its honorary presidents.

At the Congress of Europe, held in May 1948, it was agreed to set up a Council of Europe, to be based on economic and political union, and to include its own European assembly.

The federalists clearly hoped that the Council of Europe would be the first step towards a European Federation, but they were to be disappointed. The Council which was founded in Strasbourg in May 1949 involved no surrender of national authority. Its decisions were to be taken by unanimous not by majority voting and, as a result of British and Scandinavian influence, the new assembly was to be a consultative one only, drawn from among the members of national parliaments. Although the Council did and still does much useful work in cultural and educational fields and for human rights, it proved too weak to be an instrument for progress towards European integration.

The negotiations for setting up the Council of Europe brought out the deep differences which existed between the political outlook of Britain and those of her neighbours in mainland Europe. Britain's war-time experience had been very different from theirs. She had not been occupied or defeated by an enemy power. As head of the Commonwealth, Britain still believed in her ability to play a world role, by acting as an intermediary between the two great post-war powers, the United States and the Soviet Union.

Churchill had described Britain as operating within three interlocking and overlapping circles of relationship: Western Europe, the United States and the Commonwealth. This could give her a uniquely important position in the world and must not be sacrificed. In Britain too, the European federalists were regarded by many as unworldly idealists, using the idea of a regional federation as a step towards world government. The leaders of the Labour Party were suspicious of the capitalistic, free market forces which they believed would be entrenched in any European supranational movement. Even Churchill's own attitude towards Europe, as well as that of his Conservative colleagues, was probably misinterpreted in Europe. Writing of European federalism before the war he had said 'We are linked, but not comprised . . . We are with Europe but not of it. We are interested and associated, but not absorbed.'[3]

The post-war division of Europe

During the 1920s, supporters of European unification took it for granted that the Europe they would unite would stretch from the Atlantic seaboard in the West to the Ural Mountains of Russia in the East. In 1945, many Europeans still hoped, with General de Gaulle, the French war-time leader in exile, to see some form of all-European association 'between Slavs, Germans, Gauls and Latins'.[4] Such a union would carry great authority in world affairs and make sense in terms of industrial production and the use of economic resources. But their hopes, disappointed by Britain's lukewarm attitude to European unification, were to be destroyed by the tensions of the 'Cold War'.

In 1945, the economic situation of Europe required immediate action. Quite apart from the losses of life which had been suffered and the problems of Europe's nine million refugees, towns, roads and railways had been destroyed by war-time bombing. Capital investment in industry had been neglected except for military purposes. The iron, steel, coal, chemicals, bricks and cement now needed urgently for reconstruction were in short supply and industry was unable to produce the exports needed to pay for imported goods from the United States.

A war-time agency had been set up in 1943 to help with economic reconstruction in the occupied countries of Europe and in 1947 it was taken over by the United Nations Economic Commission. But already cooperation between the Soviet Union and the Western powers was coming to an end. Soviet ambitions in Eastern Europe, her need for reparations to replace her immense war losses and for her security, had soured relations between the United States and the Soviet Union. By 1946, Soviet-dominated Communist regimes were established either by force or by intense political pressure in Eastern Europe, from the Baltic Sea to the Adriatic. The 1947 American Marshall Plan, offering economic aid 'To support free peoples who are resisting attempted subjugation by armed minorities, or by outside pressure', was accepted by the governments of Western Europe, but rejected by the Soviet Union, and by Poland, Hungary, and Czechoslovakia, who saw it as a dangerous opportunity for the United States to use political pressure. Europe was soon to be divided into two hostile camps, by the followers of two apparently irreconcilable political ideologies, Communism and pluralist-democracy. Future attempts at peaceful cooperation, let alone European unification, would have to be confined to Western Europe.

Economic cooperation in Western Europe

Sixteen Western European governments established the Organisation for European Economic Cooperation (OEEC) in June 1948, to administer the American aid programme and to cooperate in helping European economic recovery. The OEEC encouraged the abolition of tariffs and other trade barriers between the member states. It led to the creation of a European Payments Union, a multilateral clearing house for monetary transfers. It was hoped that the OEEC would develop into a permanent organisation for Western European cooperation but through Britain and Scandinavian influence again it remained an intergovernmental organisation, with no supranational institutions. It did not satisfy the federalists, in particular Jean Monnet, who still hoped to introduce at European level the kind of institutions based on 'neo-functionalist' principles, which he had already helped to introduce into French post-war economic planning.

Jean Monnet and economic planning

Jean Monnet, now remembered as the most influential of the 'founding fathers' of the European Economic Community, had already had a distinguished career as an international administrator in the years between the wars. At the height of the crisis caused by the defeat of the French army in 1940 he persuaded Churchill to propose an Anglo-French Union, a joint army, a single Parliament and a full union of the two powers. When the fall of France put an end to these plans, Monnet went to Washington as General de Gaulle's representative in Anglo-American economic negotiations.

By 1943 Monnet was already urging that after the war the tariff barriers and frontiers of Europe should be abolished: 'If the states were reconstructed on a basis of national sovereignty involving as it would, policies of prestige and economic protection...' peace would be illusory. 'They must have larger markets... their prosperity and the indispensable social developments are impossible unless the States of Europe form themselves into a Federation or a "European Entity" which will make of it a common economic unit.'[5]

Economists between the wars had already noted the growing disparities between European and American industrial growth. In the United States, with its continental-wide market, industrial production had increased by 163 per cent between 1900 and 1938.[6] In 1913 the countries of Western Europe had produced roughly one-half of the world's industrial goods. Forty years later Western Europe's share had dropped to little more than a quarter and had been overtaken by that of North America. The classical economists had claimed that a larger market leads to economies of scale in mass-production and distribution, and hence to lower costs. Large-scale producers have easier access to sources of capital, while wider competition stimulates technical improvement and modernisation of plant. Increased specialisation and the economic location of industries are made possible. The success of the American big business corporations founded by Ford, Rockefeller and Carnegie in the early years of the twentieth century seemed to prove the point. Monnet was among those who recognised that in post-war Europe the introduction of modern financial organisation and new technology from the USA would lead inevitably to the creation of larger industrial units and groupings.

The Second World War had impressed upon Western European governments the need for more detailed planning controls and for governments to take a far more central role in the direction of national economies. In the post-war world the state would have to continue to take greater responsibility for economic affairs, through labour laws and through the restraint or stimulation of the economy by means of taxation policy, subsidies and monetary controls. In France in 1946 Monnet was put in charge of the modernisation and re-equipment of French industry. With a small group of colleagues who included Pierre Uri and Etienne Hirsch he established the *Commissariat au*

Plan, through which directors of national enterprises and private companies, trade union leaders and civil servants were brought together to plan production according to the country's needs. All the basic sectors of the French economy – mines, transport, electricity, steel – were to be developed according to overall national requirements.

By the late 1940s when the economies of most Western European countries were on the way to recovery, it was becoming clear that dramatic changes in the scale of the economic problems of Europe were taking place. To Monnet and his colleagues joint international economic planning had become essential. It no longer seemed possible to achieve the economies of scale, marketing, research and technological development necessary for economic survival on a purely national basis.

The Benelux Customs Union

A successful example of economic integration already existed in Europe. In 1944, Belgium, the Netherlands and Luxembourg had agreed to form a Customs Union. From January 1948 all tariffs between the three members were abolished. A single tariff was imposed on imports from outside the Union and the member states undertook to try to harmonise their economic policies. 'Benelux' proved to be a successful and smooth-running arrangement.

Monnet, with his insistence that cooperation across national frontiers and eventual European federation should begin with specific functional activities, supported a gradual sector-by-sector approach. Integration of one sector of national economies would lead on to other activities, and cooperation over technical and economic matters would be the first step towards joint political decision-making.

Political events gave further proof to Monnet that his approach was the right one. The Americans decided to build up West Germany as a defence against the threat from the Soviet Union, rather than, as had been intended during the war, to de-industralise it and keep it weak. A West German Government was set up in 1949 and the Ruhr industries were handed back to Germany. The Saarland, the German-speaking coal-producing area attached to France since 1947, was granted political autonomy, though remaining in economic union with France. French political leaders were thoroughly alarmed by the prospect of a German revival. Monnet therefore proposed that the

Rhine coalfields and iron and steel industries should be run by an independent European authority. In this way the 'containment' of Germany could be combined with the first step towards the proposed European federation. Other 'sector' integration, for example agriculture and transport, was to follow.

The European Coal and Steel Community

Monnet's proposal was received with enthusiasm. Robert Schuman, the French Foreign Minister, a Lorraine Frenchman, born in Luxembourg and educated in Germany, put forward plans for the pooling of coal and steel production. The West German Chancellor, Konrad Adenauer, a Rhineland Catholic, eager for Germany to re-establish herself in Europe and to end Franco-German hostility; the Austrian-born Italian Prime Minister, Alcide de Gasperi; the Benelux statesmen Paul-Henri Spaak, J.W. Beyen and Joseph Bech, were all committed to the European idea.

After long negotiations, the Schuman Plan was adopted by France, West Germany, Italy, Belgium, Luxembourg and the Netherlands, whose governments agreed to join the European Coal and Steel Community (ECSC), and signed the Treaty of Paris in April 1951.

The High Authority of the Coal and Steel Community was the kind of institution that the federalists had been aiming for. Its nine members, drawn from each of the member states but independent of their governments, were given real powers to enforce decisions about the management of the coal and steel industries throughout the Community. It could remove tariffs and other barriers to the movement of coal and steel. In addition to the High Authority, a Court of Justice to interpret the Treaty and to punish breaches of it, a Council of Ministers to represent the national member governments and an assembly of members delegated from national parliaments were set up. Luxembourg became the seat of the Community's institutions and Jean Monnet was appointed first president of the High Authority.

Britain was not a signatory to the Treaty of Paris. Neither Britain nor the Scandinavian countries were prepared to accept the 'supranational' nature of the new authority. In Britain the coal industry had already been nationalised and negotiations were under way to nationalise steel. The Labour Government mistrusted the free enterprise nature of European industry. Britain's absence was a handicap to the ECSC since at that time she produced half the coal and one-third of the steel output of Europe. By 1953 she had an association agreement with the Community, but her failure to become a full member marked the beginning of a divergence of ways between Britain and the six Community states which allowed France to take over the political leadership of Western Europe during the 1960s.

By 1958 when the initial transition period ended, a common market in coal and steel had been established between the member states. All customs tariffs and quotas had been abolished and policy-making for the coal and steel industries had been transferred to the Community institutions. The Belgian coal and Italian steel industries were being given help to overcome the impact of competition. Inter-state trading in coal had grown by 21 per cent, in iron ore by over 25 per cent and in steel by 157 per cent. It was a time of optimism for the supporters of integration who hoped to move from sectoral integration into wider fields. The next attempt, to establish a defence and a political community, was less successful.

The failure of the European Defence and Political Communities

A system of defensive military alliances was established in Western Europe in the years following the Second World War. It was intended at first to be a safeguard against a revival of German militarism, and later was developed in response to fears of Soviet aggression. It included the Brussels Treaty Organisation, established between Britain, France, Belgium, the Netherlands and Luxembourg in 1948.

The founding of the Cominform by the Soviet Union in 1947, the part played by her in imposing a Communist regime in Czechoslovakia, and the Berlin air blockade of 1948–49 all combined to bring the Americans, together with Canada, into the defence system of Western Europe, through the North Atlantic Pact of April 1949.

None of these alliances involved the surrender of national authority to a supranational organisation. Political control over their own armed forces remained with each member state. But after the outbreak of the Korean War in 1950, the United States proposed that West Germany, now once again a sovereign state, should contribute to European defence. Neither the new Federal Republic, nor France, was happy with the proposal, and French fears of a renewal of German militarism led to their 1950 Pleven Plan for a European Defence Community, with a European army, including German units, to be controlled by a European ministry of defence responsible to a European assembly.

Once again British support was lacking. Despite a speech by Churchill in the Council of Europe in August 1950 calling for 'the creation of a European Army under the authority of a European Minister of Defence, subject to European democratic control', Britain declined to become a member of the Defence Community. She could offer, in Foreign Minister Anthony Eden's words 'the closest possible association',[7] but not full membership. Britain again refused to commit herself fully to a European role.

French opinion, already worried by the possibility of losing control over their own national army within a European force, was undoubtedly influenced by the British attitude. The European Defence Treaty was rejected by the French Assembly, although already ratified in West Germany, Belgium, Holland and Luxembourg.

A parallel proposal for a European Political Union was abandoned at the same time. Paul-Henri Spaak had proposed that the institutions of the European Coal and Steel Community and of the Defence Community should be combined into one Political Community, with a European Executive Council and an elected President, a Parliament with a directly elected Peoples Chamber and an indirectly elected Senate, and a Council of Ministers and a Court of Justice.

The proposals for a European Defence Community and a European Political Union marked the highest point of the influence of the post-war federal movement on European politics. At no time since have the circumstances or the political will of the member states allowed such far-reaching measures to be tried again. The new post-war constitutions of Western Europe, of the Fourth French Republic founded in 1946, the Italian Republic of 1947, the West German Federal Republic of 1949 and the Netherlands of 1953 had all provided for the transfer of some national authority to a future European Union. But, from 1953 onwards, the urgency of the need for European unity began to decline. The immediate post-war fears, which had provided the stimulus for the movement towards European federation, were over. A gradual thaw in the 'Cold War' set in. Over the next ten years détente developed between East and West. The Test Ban Treaty of 1963 and the Non-Proliferation Treaty in 1968 were to prepare the way for Henry Kissinger's policy of cooperation between the United States and the Soviet Union in the 1970s. The Atlantic Alliance survived the failure of the European Defence Treaty, and in 1954 the Brussels Treaty Organisation was enlarged to include West Germany and Italy and was renamed the Western European Union. Germany was re-armed within the Brussels Treaty Organisation and showed no signs of a return to militarism. Britain hoped that the Western European Union would develop beyond defence to become a forum for regular political and economic consultation, but it was always intended that control of it should remain firmly in the hands of the national governments.

The foundation of the Economic Community

Economic recovery in Western Europe was beginning to restore confidence in the efficiency of the nation state as a political unit. Functional cooperation between the member states no longer seemed so urgent. But Monnet thought it imperative that those who believed in a politically united Europe should retake the initiative. In November 1954 he resigned from the Presidency of the High Authority of the Coal and Steel Community to work for the 'relance', the relaunching of the movement towards European unification. An Action Committee for the United States of Europe was founded. Among the political leaders in the six member countries of the Coal and Steel Community who were to become members were Guy Mollet, Maurice Faure, Willy Brandt, Aldo Moro and René Pleven.

Monnet was still in favour of a sectoral approach to European unification and he hoped to make the nuclear power industry the next sector for integration, but in the Benelux countries it was widely felt that a more general form of economic integration was needed to revive public interest in the idea of eventual political union. Free trade between the member states should lead on to a closer union, at first in terms of economics, later by a 'spill-over' effect into politics. By creating a larger, tariff-free market, eliminating non-tariff barriers to trade, and taking other steps to ensure fair competition between the partners, higher living standards and increased political stability would be bound to result.

A meeting of Foreign Ministers of the six was held in Messina, Sicily, in 1955, and it was agreed, with surprisingly little opposition, to accept in principle a Dutch proposal 'to work for the establishment of a united Europe by the development of common institutions, the progressive fusion of national economies, the creation of a common market and the progressive harmonisation of social policies'.

An intergovernmental committee under the Chairmanship of Paul-Henri Spaak, the Belgian Foreign Minister, began examining ways of finding 'a fresh advance towards the building of Europe'. It suggested a two-pronged approach: the setting up of a general common market and a further attempt at sectoral integration, namely the joint development of nuclear energy for peaceful purposes.

Customs Union and Common Market

During the 1950s, the customs frontier had become a symbol of the divisions between the countries of Europe. Pro-European groups of demonstrators had marched on frontier posts and overturned the barriers. The Spaak Committee proposed that a full customs union should be the cornerstone of European unification. The removal of internal customs duties and the erection of a common external tariff around the enlarged market would be followed by moves towards the creation of a 'common market'. Through the establishment of freedom of movement for workers and capital, Community citizens would be allowed to settle anywhere within the Community, to carry out their trade or profession. A range of common policies, for example, in agriculture, transport and taxation would be introduced. Rules for eliminating monopolies, for protecting underdeveloped regions and to help declining industries would establish conditions of genuine competition throughout the Community. Common institutions would be necessary to control these activities.

It was clear that proposals to establish a common external tariff and to set up common institutions would not be acceptable to Great Britain, with her continuing Commonwealth links and her dislike of supranational institutions. Although the United Kingdom, as well as the original members of the Coal and Steel Community took part in the preliminary talks, her representation was soon withdrawn from the negotiations which began in Brussels.

The remaining group of six states had already demonstrated within the Coal and Steel Community that they could work together. They were relatively similar in size and level of economic development and they had comparable political systems, all of which seemed to indicate that together they could form the core of a regional community. With the rejection of the European Defence Community proposals by the French Assembly still in mind, the French negotiating team were allowed to dominate the Brussels talks. The outlines of a common agricultural policy which would be advantageous to French agriculture were agreed upon, and arrangements were made for development aid to be given to France's overseas possessions. West Germany welcomed the prospect through membership of a greatly expanded tariff-free market for her industrial goods and a return to international political respectability. Italy was to receive help for the Mezzogiorno, the backward southern half of the country, whose problems threatened her political stability. The smaller Benelux countries had always felt that they would make considerable commercial gains from such a grouping, as well as gaining a more influential voice in international affairs.

On 27 March 1957, the Treaties creating the European Economic Community (EEC) and the European Atomic Energy Community (Euratom), to develop the use of nuclear energy for peaceful purposes, were signed in Rome, to come into operation on 1 January 1958. By accepting the Treaty of Rome, the member states agreed to work together to bring about an integrated multinational economy, within which there would eventually be free movement of labour and of capital, rules to prevent the distortion of the market, joint institutions and common policies towards underdeveloped regions of the Community and towards the outside world. Moreover, in its intentions, the Treaty of Rome was implicitly political. Its preamble clearly stated that it was intended to 'lay the foundations of an ever closer union among the peoples of Europe'.

2 The Economic Community 1958-73

The Treaty of Rome

When the Communities were founded it was at first thought that of the two new organisations, Euratom would be the more active. Nuclear energy seemed an ideal industry for joint development at European level. With Community-wide planning and research, it was hoped that the industry would be able to provide Europe with plentiful cheap energy resources. But, during the 1960s, national governments became increasingly reluctant to lose control of their own nuclear research programmes. Britain's absence, and the advanced technical knowledge which she could have contributed, was also a blow to the development of a joint nuclear energy programme. But although Euratom failed to develop, the Economic Community established itself rapidly during the 1960s.

The Treaty of Rome was the outcome of hard bargaining and of a series of compromises between the negotiators. Much of it took the form of a framework for future action. Only over the Customs Union were firm dates given, and procedures and duties clearly stated. Certain common policies, for agriculture and for transport, for example, were to be worked out fully once the Communities were established, but general aims and overall timetables for implementing these policies were laid down in the Treaty.

The institutions set up by the Treaty, though similar to those of the European Coal and Steel Community, were less 'supranational'; the member states were no longer prepared to give up substantial national powers to an organisation with independent authority, especially one which was to operate over a much wider field than that of the Coal and Steel Community. The Commission of the Economic Community, like the High Authority of the ECSC, was independent of the member state governments. Its nine members, two each from France, Italy and West Germany and one from each of the Benelux countries, were appointed by the national governments, but during their term in office were responsible only to the European Assembly. Its functions were similar to those of the High Authority of the Coal and Steel Community for initiating policy and for putting into action, but it was given no legislative powers, nor control over the Community budget. The right to legislate was to be in the hands of an intergovernmental Council composed of one Minister from each of the member states, but in order to ensure that decision-making should become progressively more 'supranational', voting procedures in the Council were to switch gradually on an increasing number of issues from unanimity to weighted majority voting. A European Court of Justice was to provide the necessary legal sanctions for carrying out the Treaty. A European Assembly, made up at first of nominated members from the national parliaments, was eventually to be elected directly by universal suffrage. Its part in the legislative process was to be an advisory one only and originally it had no budgetary control, though the Treaty authors intended that the authority of the Assembly should gradually increase.

Once the Common External Tariff had come into operation, the Community was to be financed directly from its own resources.

Establishing the Customs Union

Between 1958 and 1962, a favourable economic situation and the support given to the Community by the United States, which regarded it as a possible counterweight to Soviet influence in Europe, gave the Community a promising start. Backed by American nuclear protection, and with the US dollar to provide an effective medium of exchange and a reserve currency, the Community itself was able to concentrate on achieving its economic objectives.

A twelve-year transitional period had been allowed by the Treaty for the achievement of the Customs Union. The first internal tariff cuts were made in 1959, and were followed by moves towards formulating a common agricultural policy. A European Social Fund was set up to deal with cases of hardship caused by the change-over to Community-wide planning and production. A European Investment Bank was established through which loans could be advanced to companies, enterprises and financial institutions across national frontiers where necessary.

Progress towards establishing the Customs Union was made by way of bargaining between the representatives of the member states and the negotiation of 'package deals', which gave some benefit to each. Agreements were often reached only after marathon all-night sessions of the Council of Ministers; a procedure which has become almost standard for Community decision-making. Nevertheless, by 1 July 1968 all internal tariffs had been abolished between the member states, and the Common External Tariff came into force, well ahead of schedule.

The Customs Union is the foundation upon which the Economic Community was built. But the Community was also aiming at the establishment of a common market. Many factors apart from tariffs can obstruct the flow of trade and divide a market. The long, slow process began of eliminating these impediments to trade. It still takes up much of the time of the Community Commission's staff in Brussels.

Eliminating non-tariff barriers to trade

The Economic Community is based upon an acceptance of Community-wide production and distribution of products and services as a development of the industrial economy which should make a valuable contribution to economic growth and prosperity. One of the declared objectives of the Common Market was to help cross-frontier mergers and the amalgamation of undertakings. At the same time the Community needed to take measures to guard against restrictive practices, excessive concentration and the abuse of dominant industrial positions.

Restrictive arrangements between firms (cartels) can take various forms. They may be price-fixing arrangements through which enterprises agree the prices which they charge on exports to other member states; or agreements between firms to create common selling syndicates, to conduct the sales of particular products. Other restrictive practices include agreements between firms to reserve specified markets, quota agreements through which firms agree not to overstock a market, reciprocal dealing arrangements which make it impossible for outside suppliers to penetrate a market and mergers or take-overs which create conditions of dominance or monopoly in a particular area.

Articles 85–90 of the Treaty of Rome were drawn up to deal with restrictive practices which might affect Community trade and impede the progress of integration. In this sphere, the Treaty gave the Community institutions considerable specific powers. Under regulations introduced from 1962 onwards, enterprises must notify certain restrictive agreements to the competition Directorate-General of the Commission in Brussels. The Commission can make formal decisions, granting clearances or exemptions, or can prohibit such agreements. It may take proceedings against firms on its own initiative, or act on complaints received and it may impose fines if necessary.

State aids to enterprises may also distort competition and are forbidden by the Treaty, unless they can be shown to be needed because of social or economic hardship, or are of European-wide benefit. Regional aids or help to industries which contribute to the balanced development of the Community may be exempted from the Treaty rulings.

The harmonisation of national standards and laws

All governments lay down rules for the standard and quality of the goods sold on their national markets. These standards are normally intended to protect the public against possible injury or deception. Legislation already existed in all the member states, regulating colouring and preserving agents in food, laying down safety standards for electrical equipment, drug content, braking and lighting systems in motor vehicles, for example. But if national standards differ widely between states, then they may become obstacles to trade between countries. Widely disparate rates of taxation and standards of professional qualifications, for instance, can interfere with the right granted by the Treaty for citizens to earn their living anywhere they wish within the Community. Professional diplomas and educational qualifications are to be recognised and accepted in all the member states.

The Treaty therefore gave the Community institutions powers to take any necessary steps to adjust national legal rules, through harmonisation procedures, in order to remove national, technical or legal arrangements which could inhibit the development of a common market, through preventing the free movement of products, people and resources. Harmonisation activities cover an enormously wide area and work on harmonisation will continue for many years. Commission Directorates-General which are among those constantly occupied with harmonisation measures include Financial Institutions and Taxation, Industrial Affairs and Research, Science and Education.

The Common Agricultural Policy

During the ten years following the signing of the Treaty of Rome, the development of the common agricultural market became almost synonymous with the progress of the Community itself and the Common Agricultural Policy is still the Community's most important single practical achievement.

There were a number of reasons why it was thought necessary to work out a Community agricultural policy in detail, whereas for industrial products only the barriers to trade were to be removed. A secure food supply and a prosperous agricultural industry were considered to be an essential basis for economic prosperity. If food prices and agricultural costs were allowed to differ widely in each Community country, free trade in manufactured goods would be undermined too. But methods of subsidising and protecting agriculture were extremely complicated, far more so than similar measures for manufacturing industries. In Britain where plentiful food supplies had been assured in the past by the colonies and dominions, the emphasis in agricultural policy was on cheap food, rather than on security of supply. In Continental Europe, the traditional emphasis had always been on self-sufficiency, and agriculture was protected by quota arrangements, guaranteed prices and export subsidies. Britain's farming industry was small, efficient and relatively advanced in technology, but in most of Europe peasant farmers still worked small and inefficient farms and incomes were falling behind those of industrial workers. In Britain in the late 1950s only 4 per cent of the working population was in farming, but in the six countries which joined the Community in 1958, 17½ million people were still living off the land, one-quarter of the total working population, and their incomes were only half those in other industries. France in particular, with 23 per cent of her working population still engaged in agriculture and with many problems caused by isolated farming communities and small, fragmented farms, had a powerful farming lobby. The Community agricultural policy which emerged was largely designed to meet French interests.

It was accepted that a common policy would be needed, which would enable the Community to increase farm productivity rapidly while allowing producers to remain in business with an adequate income and maintaining regular supplies of food at reasonable prices to consumers. The Common Agricultural Policy (CAP) therefore had three main objectives: to establish a single Community market in agricultural products, with common agricultural prices throughout the Community; to maintain Community preference against suppliers from outside the Community; and to ensure that the costs of the policy should be met by the Community as a whole.

First, the 'unity of the market' was established by fixing Community-level common standards and prices at levels judged to be appropriate to give adequate incomes to producers. Where market prices fall below this level, the Community intervenes to buy up surpluses and to maintain guaranteed prices. The surplus is stored until it can be sold back to the market, or it is exported or subsidised for sale to schools, hospitals or pensioners within the Community. Community products are protected from cheaper imports and from the effects of fluctuations in world market prices by a system of border levies and 'entry' prices mechanisms which trigger off import levies when prices outside the Community fall below Community price levels.

Under the Common Agricultural Policy, as in the Customs Union, the Community has developed its own powers of management and negotiation. Each member state accepts the financial consequences of decisions taken by the Community's Agricultural Council. A European Agricultural Guidance and Guarantee Fund, administered by the Community Commission, meets the cost of the policy. The Guarantee Section finances marketing and price policies, including intervention buying and the cost of export and consumer subsidies and the Guidance Section helps with modernisation schemes and measures to reduce income differences between farmers in different parts of the Community, and between farming and other industries.

The common organisation of individual agricultural markets was introduced gradually throughout the 1960s and common farm prices were finally agreed in 1967. The question of financing the Common Agricultural Policy had caused bitter disagreements over whether the Community institutions should be allowed full responsibility for the huge sums of money involved. Final agreement was reached only at the cost of abandoning the principle of decision-making by majority voting in the Council of Ministers, thus in practice allowing the French a veto on agricultural matters. Community financing of agricultural expenditure was complete by 1968.

The achievements of the first ten years
During the first ten years of its existence, when the Community con-

centrated almost entirely on economic and commercial matters, its economic achievements were substantial. They were acknowledged by the figures given in a British Government White Paper, published in 1971, just before the debate in the Westminster Parliament on British entry into Europe.[1]

The EEC, it concluded, had created an environment in which great economic progress had been made. The abolition of tariffs had encouraged mutual trade, so that by 1969 intra-Community trade in manufactured products was about 50 per cent higher than it would have been if there had been no Community. Stronger competition had forced industries to seek more efficient, lower-cost, production methods. Prospects for exporting had improved rapidly, together with investment growth. In real terms, British earnings had increased by less than 40 per cent between 1958–69, whereas in the Community countries real earnings had increased by more than 75 per cent. In all the Community countries, the rate of growth of gross national product (GNP) per head of population was twice that of Britain's. Between 1959–69, 24 per cent of the Community countries' GNP went to investment, compared to 17 per cent in the United Kingdom. The Community countries earned a surplus of more than $25,000 m. in 1958–69 on their balance of payments, whilst the United Kingdom had a small deficit over the same period.

A report published by the European Community itself in 1972[2] analysed the achievements of the Community in terms of evolution of structures of production, abolition of trade barriers, rise in incomes and living standards, stability of expansion and the contribution made by the Community to the world economic order. Its findings showed an average yearly growth of GNP of 5.7 per cent and an increase in per capita income and consumption of about 4.5 per cent per annum. Industry's contribution to GNP had increased in all the member states, while that of agriculture had been halved.

It seemed unlikely that the Six could have made independently the impressive economic progress they had achieved as a group. The Community appeared to be offering a more appropriate level for tackling modern production needs, in terms of labour, capital and industrial location. The larger market allowed for more rational use to be made of resources and for higher productivity.

Each of the member states appeared to have benefited from Community membership. The German Federal Republic was politically stable and its economy was thriving after an almost miraculous post-war recovery. French agriculture had benefited, as expected, from the agricultural policy. Italy was receiving help in dealing with the problems of the poverty-stricken Mezzogiorno and was more stable politically. The Benelux countries had gained commercially. In Belgium, Flanders had grown from an underdeveloped into an industrial region in the Community's heartland, and Belgium as a whole had gained from the many international companies which had set up their European headquarters there. The Netherlands had also benefited from the common agricultural policy and the extensive development of the port of Rotterdam was one indication of the great growth in Dutch trade. Luxembourg, the site of the first headquarters of the Community, had gained considerably from the many new jobs it had created.

Internal support for the Community was growing in each country. In addition to the relatively small group of politicians, civil servants, businessmen and trade union leaders who had pressed for the establishment of the Economic Community, national administrators too were finding themselves increasingly involved in the Community's procedures and decisions.

Party political acceptance of the Community was spreading right across the political spectrum. By 1969, not only the right-wing German and Italian Christian Democratic parties and the French MRP, the moderate French Radical party, German FDP and the Liberals and Monarchists in Italy, who had backed the Community from the beginning, but the moderate left, the Social Democrats in the Benelux countries, France, Italy and West Germany, and the Italian Socialists were represented in the European Assembly, together with the French and Italian Communist parties who had earlier shown considerable opposition to the European Community.* The Christian and Free Trade Unions had also accepted the idea of economic integration.

Externally, the Community was becoming recognised as a new framework for economic and political relationships. The Customs Union gave the Community the opportunity to speak as one in international trade relations and to act as a single negotiator, while neighbouring states were increasingly interested in joining, or making trade agreements, with the Community.

* Attitudes of European political parties towards the Community are examined more fully on pp. 89–92.

Its institutions had developed a range of procedures which, though slow and complicated, could achieve agreement on certain policies. Though not developing in the way hoped for by the federalist 'founding fathers' of the Community, they had at least demonstrated that they could survive crises. But, after 1966, there was something of an institutional deadlock in the Community and little progress was made towards introducing further policies before the early 1970s.

However, the Common Agricultural Policy, based on self-sufficiency, achieved through guaranteed prices to farmers and secure markets, had developed further and more rapidly than other common policies. Agricultural trade had quadrupled between the Six in ten years. By 1968 self-sufficiency had been achieved in many products, including milk, eggs, beef and poultry. By 1972 the number of farmers in the Community had been almost halved yet agricultural productivity had been increased. But the cost of these achievements was high and some of the objectives of the policy were not reached. Agricultural efficiency was still low compared to that of Britain, the United States, Canada, Australia or New Zealand. Many of the criticisms which have been levelled against the Common Agricultural Policy were stated forcefully at the time of British entry into the Community in 1973 and the CAP has remained a controversial Community issue, particularly in Britain.†

† See pp. 143–8 for further discussion of the CAP.

3 The Community and Political Issues during the 1960s

Britain and the European Free Trade Area

In the late 1950s Britain, although eager to return to freer trade, could not accept the 'institutional market' which the Europeans were proposing to introduce. She could not agree to an agricultural common market which would exclude Commonwealth exports and her preferential arrangements with them. The Customs Union and the internal free trade area of the Community would threaten her own industrial exports.

Britain during the 1950s was still trying to play the world role to which she had become accustomed as head of an Empire. But her attempts at 'summit' diplomacy had alienated both West Germany under Adenauer's leadership, and successive governments in France. In 1956, the failure of the United States to support her at the time of her clash with Nasser's Egypt over the nationalisation of the Suez Canal, had shown up her growing isolation.

In 1957, Harold Macmillan made an attempt to take back the leadership of Europe with a scheme to create a European-wide free trade area in industrial goods. Negotiations were begun to try to link eleven countries outside the new Economic Community with the six member states in a looser association than that of a customs union. Tariffs would be dismantled between the member states, but separate national tariffs towards the outside world would be maintained. In 1958 General de Gaulle returned to power in France. He rejected Britain's proposals, on the grounds that a British-dominated free trade area 'would drown the infant Community·in a vast sea of free trade'.[1] He accused Britain of trying to take advantage of the larger market created by the Economic Community, without accepting the obligation of working within the institutions. De Gaulle himself had every intention of using the Economic Community to strengthen France's political position in Europe. He began to develop closer relations between France and

West Germany, offering support to West Germany over its claims to West Berlin and the prospect of the restoration of German national sovereign rights. In return, the Germans were to back a French-dominated Community, with its advantages for French agriculture, from which Britain would be excluded.

The European Free Trade Area (EFTA) was set up in November 1959 between Britain and six other OEEC member states which had not joined the Economic Community: Norway, Denmark, Sweden, Switzerland, Austria and Portugal. (At the same time OEEC was replaced by the OECD, a mainly advisory and research organisation, with Canada and the United States as additional members.) EFTA covered industrial trade only, with no provisions for agriculture and no institutional framework. Since there was to be no common external tariff, Britain would be free to maintain her preferential Commonwealth arrangements.

EFTA, though effective, did not achieve the success of the Economic Community. It was in no sense a political organisation, more a commercial arrangement, and its economic and social resources were much smaller. Before long it became a means of holding its members together while they negotiated terms of entry into the Economic Community. It did not help Britain to regain the political initiative in Europe, which for the next few years remained with France. After Britain and Denmark joined the Economic Community in 1973, the remaining EFTA members, which by that time also included Iceland, together with Finland as an associate member, signed association agreements with the Community, creating by 1977 the largest industrial free trade area in the world.

Britain's first attempt to join the Community
By 1960, the Community's economic growth rate was already two and-a-half times as fast as that of Britain and it was becoming obvious that Britain's economy could no longer maintain the financial burden of attempting to play a world-wide role. Her Commonwealth links were weakening and the United States government was anxious for her to join and strengthen the European Community, which it saw as a safeguard against Communism and domestic instability.

In 1961, Macmillan announced Britain's intention of applying for Community membership, on the grounds of the economic advantages it offered. His personal ascendancy was such that he was able to carry his party with him, against the mainstream of Conservative thought at that time. Strong disagreement over the question of British membership, and clashes between France and the rest of the Community over ways in which the Community was to develop, were to hold back the Community's political development throughout the 1960s.

Crisis over British membership

If the British found the supranational elements of the Economic Community unacceptable, de Gaulle did so no less. The long-term implications of the acceptance of the Rome Treaty: a system of majority voting among the representatives of the national governments in the Council; a supranational bureaucracy over which national governments would have little control; a directly elected European Parliament and a commitment to work for closer union, were as distasteful to President de Gaulle and to his successor Georges Pompidou as they were to the British. De Gaulle, however, was prepared to use the Community to gain political advantages for France. He planned to keep economic and social affairs apart from political issues. The Community could be allowed some responsibilities for the 'low' policy areas of economic and social affairs; but only national governments could deal with 'high' policy political issues. In 1959 de Gaulle proposed the extension of integration to defence and foreign policy, through the French Fouchet proposals for a political union, but the new institutions were to be purely intergovernmental, with regular meetings between Foreign Ministers and permanent committees on, for example, foreign policy and defence, drawn from experts in the member states. The proposals were abandoned when the Dutch, wary of possible attempts by France to undermine the Community's institutions in Brussels and conscious of difficulties with NATO and the United States, refused to take part in any discussions unless Britain was admitted to them. In 1963, de Gaulle and Adenauer signed a Franco-German Treaty of Cooperation. De Gaulle's plans for a confederal *Europe des patries* were to be based on close Franco-German cooperation, detached from the Atlantic Alliance.

The first formal British application for membership, in August 1961, and those of Denmark, Ireland and Norway, were followed by a series of negotiations during the following year, with Edward Heath heading the British negotiating team. But the Nassau Conference in December 1962, at which the United States offered Britain American

Polaris missiles, had convinced de Gaulle that Britain was too closely linked to the United States to become a member of the European Community. By using his right of veto in the Community's Council of Ministers he brought the entry negotiations to an abrupt halt. His reasons were given at a press conference in Paris in January 1963: 'England is, in effect, insular, maritime, linked through its trade, markets and food supply to very diverse and often very distant countries.' If Britain entered the Community 'in the end there would appear a colossal Atlantic Community under American dependence and leadership which would soon completely swallow up the European Community'.[2] Little consultation with the other Community countries seemed to have preceded his action. When Ludwig Erhard succeeded Adenauer to the post of West German Chancellor, it became clear that the Germans intended to support American proposals for a multilateral nuclear force within the framework of NATO, whereas de Gaulle had hoped for German support for a separate French *force de frappe*. By the time France withdrew from the integrated military structure of NATO in 1966 hopes of an identity of Franco-German views on such matters had already faded.

The 1965 Community crisis
In 1965, the disagreements created by de Gaulle's view of Europe and those of the rest of the Community came to a head. Under the terms of the Treaty of Rome, decision-making by majority voting under certain issues, in the Council of Ministers, was due to come into force automatically on 1 January 1966. France was determined to oppose this.

Community administrators were in the process of working out the financial regulations for the Agricultural Policy during 1965. Their rapid completion was in the interests of French agriculture. Walter Hallstein, President of the Commission since 1958, was an ardent federalist, determined to strengthen the Community institutions and to work for further integration. The Commission proposed tying three connected issues into one 'package deal': the completion of farm price negotiations; the granting of a direct source of revenue to the Community by arranging for levies on agricultural imports to be paid directly to the Community; and, in order to ensure adequate democratic control over the large sums of money involved, the granting of greater budgetary powers to the Community Assembly.

The French angrily requested that the problem of farm finances be settled first. When the Council of Ministers refused, the French Permanent Representation was withdrawn from Brussels. In de Gaulle's view, the prospect of independent initiatives by the Commission and of increased use of majority voting in the Council of Ministers were a threat to his plans for the future of the Community. For the next seven months, French representatives refused to attend any meetings of the Council of Ministers or of its working groups. In other Community institutions, administrators continued to attend to routine matters, but no new policies could be initiated or new Community legislation passed. The Community process was effectively blocked at the level where decisions were taken.

However, the other five member states stayed firmly united in insisting that the deadlock be resolved within the Community's own framework. For the first time West German representatives in the Council took the lead in Community affairs. In the French Presidential elections of December 1965, de Gaulle's majority was considerably reduced, and his policy towards the European Community was regarded as a significant factor in his declining popularity. In January 1966 a compromise settlement was reached by the Council of Ministers.

The Luxembourg compromise

Although the Commission's right to initiate Community policy was confirmed, it was agreed that it should consult more closely in future with the member state governments before putting forward new proposals. Over the issue of majority voting in the Council of Ministers, an 'agreement to disagree' was accepted. Although majority voting on certain issues had officially come into effect from 1 January 1966, it was agreed that 'on issues very important to one or more member countries, the Council should try to reach unanimity'. The result was that the member states became unwilling to introduce controversial measures which might provoke a national veto and create similar crises. With every country in effect able to veto important legislation, a complex system of consultation began to develop between the member states. Inevitably a shift in influence took place, from the Commission to the intergovernmental Council and its Committees, at the centre of the decision-making process.

Significantly, in the Merger Treaty, which had been signed in Brussels in April 1965, officially merging the institutions of the three

Communities, the European Coal and Steel Community, the European Economic Community and Euratom (the European Court and the European Parliament already served all the three Communities), official recognition was given for the first time to the Committee of Permanent Representatives of the member states, an intergovernmental body which was to play an increasingly important role in the Community.

The 1965 crisis ended hopes for the time being of major institutional developments towards more supranational control. The questions of independent financial resources for the Community, and of increased budgetary powers for the European Parliament, were shelved indefinitely. For the time being, the Community settled down to being a Customs Union, working towards the completion of a Common Market, with some shared institutions and common policies. Little progress could be expected in initiating further common policies. However, it had survived a major political crisis, with evidence of a developing sense of unity among the five member states which had resisted French attempts to mould the Community to suit French policies. But it had now become clear that political unification was not going to be an automatic consequence of taking certain economic decisions jointly, nor of transferring administrative activities to Community institutions. The true source of political power was still the governments of the member states. Those governments, once again preoccupied with national problems, were no longer anxious to move rapidly towards the Community's goal of political union.

However, some progress was made between 1966–69. By 1 July 1968 the Customs Union and the Common Agricultural Policy were fully implemented. During the 1966–67 Kennedy Round of multinational trade negotiations which form part of the General Agreement on Tariffs and Trade (GATT), Jean Rey, then the Commissioner responsible for external trade matters negotiated on behalf of the six Community member states to obtain a reduction of tariffs on industrial goods.

Britain's second application for membership, 1967
The Labour government which had come into office in October 1964 under Harold Wilson's leadership had been forced to the conclusion, like the Conservative government before it, that Britain could no longer sustain her world role. Her influence over American policy-

making had decreased. She was deeply in debt and her East of Suez role had to be abandoned through economic necessity. Her relationship with the Commonwealth was changing fundamentally. Her trade with Commonwealth countries was in decline, while that with Community countries in Western Europe was increasing.

Membership of the European Economic Community seemed to offer Britain the best chance of restoring her political influence and of giving her the economic prosperity she needed. Somewhat ironically, de Gaulle's view of a *Europe des patries*, was in line with Britain's own desire for cooperation with the other member states, with a minimal loss of national sovereignty, but on the basis that the Community was not dominated by France's political needs. As a result of Britain's financial and monetary problems, the 'Group of Ten', international bankers, were able to influence government policies. Clearly some erosion of her prized national independence had already taken place. She was a member of over ninety international organisations which automatically involved some sharing of costs and decision-making. Many people were beginning to believe that it might after all be a good idea to enter a structured system with shared decision-making which at the same time offered considerable economic advantage. George Brown, then Foreign Secretary, and George Thomson, a Minister of State at the Foreign Office who later became one of Britain's first two Community Commissioners, were put in charge of the second British attempt to enter the European Community. Once again de Gaulle used his veto, this time before negotiations had begun, in November 1967.

The political stalemate in the Community was not ended until after the resignation of de Gaulle from the French Presidency in 1969. Under President Pompidou, France no longer looked upon the Community institutions with such suspicion. She was anxious to end her isolated position within the Community. Her uneasiness over West Germany's growing wealth and influence in Europe caused her to look more favourably on British entry, which, after all, would provide more markets for French agricultural surpluses, while the British were known to favour a confederal, rather than a federal, approach to Europe.

Elsewhere in the Community, Italy was struggling against economic instability and Belgium was preoccupied by linguistic quarrels. Willy Brandt, the Social Democratic West German Chancellor since 1969, had emerged as the most influential leader in the Community, committed both to its economic and political development and to its enlargement. In his view Britain held a key position in relation to Europe, both because of her economic, political and military history, and because of her democratic traditions. The stability of the British parliamentary system was expected to influence the Community's institutions and in particular it was hoped that British membership would speed up the emergence of an effective European parliament. He called for the reopening of negotiations with Britain and the other applicant countries, Denmark, Norway and the Irish Republic.

The 1969 Hague Conference

At the Summit Conference held in the Hague in December 1969, the leaders of the member states made a determined effort to end the period of political stagnation into which the Community had fallen. Four major decisions were taken and deadlines were set for action upon them.

The issues which had caused the 1965–66 crisis were resolved with an agreement on definitive financial arrangements for the Common Agricultural Policy and for direct financing of the Community from its own resources, to be achieved by the mid-1970s. Plans for a full economic union by 1980 were to go ahead and Pierre Werner, Prime Minister of Luxembourg, was appointed to lead a committee to work out the detailed arrangements. A committee under Jean Davignon, from the Belgian Foreign Office, was to study the steps that would be needed to achieve a common foreign policy. Lastly, negotiations were to begin immediately to extend Community membership to Great Britain and the other European countries anxious to join.

Membership at the third attempt

In June 1970, Edward Heath, the strongly pro-European Conservative leader, succeeded Harold Wilson as Prime Minister. In the General Election campaign EEC membership was not a main issue. Both major parties were committed to entry. Negotiations were opened in Luxembourg in June 1970, between the Community and the four applicant countries, with Geoffrey Rippon leading the British negotiating team.

Regional problems, questions of finance and the movement of capital, social policies and labour law (which was of particular interest in the Scandinavian countries), agricultural and fisheries policies were some of the main areas for negotiation. Commonwealth problems slowed up the negotiations considerably. Conditions for New Zealand agriculture and Commonwealth sugar production, which had received preferential treatment from Britain, took time to settle. Various forms of association with the Community had to be negotiated for the independent Commonwealth countries in Africa, the Caribbean and the Pacific, together with Community undertakings towards the Asian Commonwealth countries. Special arrangements were necessary for Australia and Canada, to cover the impact of the Common External Tariff.

The final terms of entry were tough for Britain to accept. Her contribution to the Community budget, after a transitional period, was to be £300 m. by 1978. Dismantling of internal customs duties was to be completed in stages by July 1977 and moves towards the application of the Common External Tariff were to begin in January 1974. The Common Agricultural Policy was reluctantly accepted, with certain exceptions for fishing and hill farming, and after a transitional period ending in 1977, because of the expected political and economic advantages of Community membership. To British eyes it seemed a policy designed for high-cost farmers, damaging to world trade and disregarding the needs of consumers. It was harmful to the interests of agricultural producers in the Commonwealth because it excluded their relatively cheap produce. It seemed likely to keep agricultural prices well above world levels, yet was expensive to taxpayers because of the high costs of protecting producers.

The Treaties of Accession were finally signed in Brussels on 22 January 1972, to come into effect on 1 January 1973. From that date Britain and the other new members were to participate in the Community institutions, with Britain being put on the same footing as the three largest existing member states.

The Treaties were then submitted to the national Parliaments for approval both in the existing member states and in the four applicant countries, in all of which, except for Britain, it was decided to hold referendums on the issue of Community membership.

The Irish referendum resulted in overwhelming approval; that held in Denmark was also decisive, with 63.5 per cent voting for Community membership and 36.5 per cent against. The Irish, whose Catholicism had already given them a wider European outlook, saw in the Community an opportunity to break free of their economic dependence on the United Kingdom and to find new markets for their agricultural produce. In Denmark both farmers and industrialists supported Community membership. In Norway, however, entry negotiations had encountered difficulties from the start. The issue of Community membership aroused strong emotions, and the referendum campaign was marked by fierce argument. Some feared the loss of Norway's independent identity within the Community. The country's war-time occupation by the Germans was recalled with bitterness, and much latent anti-German feeling re-surfaced. Norwegian shipping interests were strongly in favour of joining the Community, but the fishing industry was equally strongly opposed. The campaign cut across political party divisions, dividing families and friends. The result was a rejection of entry by a vote of 53 per cent to 47 per cent, and the new Community came into existence on 1 January 1973, with nine members instead of the expected ten. Norway has appeared to lose little by staying outside. Whereas the British and Community economies were competitive, Norway and Community countries had largely complementary economies. Her metals, alloys and raw materials were still important to the Community, while her high priced agricultural system would have found even EEC prices too low. Norway concluded an industrial free trade agreement with the Community and the Danes, who are fellow members of the Nordic Council (set up in 1952 to promote social and political cooperation between Denmark, Finland, Iceland, Norway and Sweden) have looked after many Scandinavian interests in Brussels. To most Norwegians, the question of Community membership is settled for many years to come.

British uneasiness

In Britain some opposition to membership remained. After the negotiation of entry terms was completed a Labour anti-market campaign had begun, led by Harold Wilson, who considered the terms negotiated by the Conservatives to be unfavourable and who was himself preoccupied with questions of party unity. In October 1971, the House of Commons voted 356–244 in favour of British entry on the government's proposed terms, but the country was now deeply divided over membership. Anti-marketeers considered that the cost of the CAP was unacceptable; they saw problems for the Commonwealth and for the regions if the negotiated terms were accepted. They called for fairer methods of Community financing and for the Westminster Parliament to keep its powers to control regional, industrial and fiscal policies.

It was clear too that public opinion generally was both unenthusiastic and ill-informed about the Community. Although a good deal of secondary legislation had already been passed to bring the United Kingdom into line with the Community and many consultative committees had already been set up which included members from the TUC, the CBI and other public bodies, the public in general was still not clearly aware of the issues involved in membership. There was strong support in the Labour Party for the holding of a referendum on Community membership, on the grounds that the Conservative government had only been mandated to negotiate the terms of entry and that the people should have had an opportunity to give their consent to them.

All three party leaders rejected the idea of a referendum, which Harold Wilson declared to be 'contrary to our traditions'. The decision was to be left to the elected representatives of the people in Parliament. In the autumn of 1972 Parliament gave its consent to the European Communities Bill, giving legal force to the Treaty, but with ominously strong opposition from Labour members. The Parliamentary Labour Party did not take up its allocation of seats in the European Parliament at Strasbourg and the TUC also decided to boycott the Community and its institutions.

Renegotiation and Referendum in Britain

On 1 January 1973 the United Kingdom officially became a full member of the European Economic Community, but as far as public opinion was concerned, the European partnership was not yet an accepted fact of British political life. In the 1974 General Election campaign, both renegotiation of the terms of entry, and the holding of a referendum on Community membership were important aspects of the Labour Party's election campaign, though the election itself was probably decided on domestic failures in industrial relations. With Labour's return to power in February 1974, Prime Minister Harold Wilson announced that renegotiation would take place and that a referendum would be held once the renegotiated terms were known.

By the time the next Summit meeting took place in Dublin in March 1975, many of the issues over which the Labour Party had demanded renegotiation in the election campaign, had already been settled or were no longer a threat. The negotiations of the Lomé agreement had cleared up many Commonwealth difficulties; proposals to harmonise rates of VAT had been abandoned and a review of the CAP had been promised. The proposed European Monetary Union, which would have meant massive transfers of political power to Brussels, was shelved indefinitely. Agreement was reached at Dublin to allow the United Kingdom certain budgetary adjustments and to permit the sale of New Zealand agricultural produce, including butter, within the Community. The Cabinet therefore recommended that Britain remain a member of the Community. But government ministers were left free to campaign against this majority decision – a unique move, showing how deeply the Labour Party was split.

The referendum campaign was fought not by the political parties as such, but by two 'umbrella' organisations, each of which received government grants to carry out the campaign. The Anti-Market National Referendum Campaign included the mainly Labour supported 'Common Market Safeguards Campaign', the Liberal 'Get Britain Out' group and the Conservative 'Anti-Common Market League'. It was supported by the Scottish and Welsh Nationalist Parties, the United Ulster Unionists, the Communist Party, the National Front and many leading trade unionists. It received some large Union contributions but in general tended to reflect both extreme left and extreme right in British public opinion.

'Britain in Europe' had the support of the majority of both the Conservative and Liberal parties and a large section of the Parliamentary Labour Party, the Cabinet and the Labour electorate. Many moderate centre politicians, including Roy Jenkins, Shirley Williams, Edward Heath and William Whitelaw, gave it their support. Marks and Spencer, ICI, and Shell were among many firms to contribute to its expenses.

The anti-marketeers warned of the possible loss of British jobs to Europe and of the prospect of food prices rising to Community country levels as a result of accepting the Common Agricultural policy.

'Britain in Europe' concentrated in its campaign on the need to strengthen the European partnership and on Britain's need to belong to a wider unit during the period of world-wide recession and economic crisis which was being experienced at that time.

The issue of national sovereignty
The issue of national sovereignty received much attention during the

campaign. In the twentieth century every state has accepted limitations upon its external sovereignty. Its rights to exercise independent action in international affairs is curtailed through its acceptance of international law and by its membership of international bodies which can limit even its internal actions. External sovereignty in the twentieth century has been described as 'the *residuum* of power which [a state] possesses within the confines laid down by international law'.[3]

In a political system like that of the United Kingdom, which has no written constitution, 'sovereignty' is also used to describe the ultimate source of authority within the state. In Britain, this internal sovereignty has by long tradition been accepted as resting with the elected representatives of the People in Parliament. In other Community countries the concept of internal sovereignty differs: for them sovereignty is shared. The constitution lays down rules about where the authority of each body begins and ends. In France, for example, President and Parliament are elected separately. The President appoints the government and a Constitutional Council guarantees legality. In Germany, a federal state, power is distributed on a regional basis, between the central government and the *Länder*, or state, governments.

Community membership meant that in some areas, British government was for the first time to be conducted on the basis of a written constitution, the Treaty of Rome, which the Westminster Parliament alone would be powerless to change, so long as membership lasted. Anthony Wedgwood Benn, the leading left-wing member of the Labour Party, wrote to his constituents in January 1975 that

... the power of the electors of Britain, through their direct representatives in Parliament, to make laws, levy taxes, change laws which the courts must uphold, and control the conduct of public affairs, has been substantially ceded to the European Community, whose Council of Ministers and Commission are neither collectively elected, nor collectively dismissed by the British people, nor even by the peoples of all the Community countries put together.

Enoch Powell, an influential right-wing politician and critic of British membership of the European Community, took much the same line. Supporters of Community membership, however, maintained that national sovereignty was not being abandoned, only that where sovereignty could no longer be exercised because it had ceased to exist at national level, it was now to be exercised jointly in a new form.

The Referendum verdict

The Referendum was held on 5 June 1975. Voting took place in sixty-eight special Referendum constituencies. The result, in a turn-out of 65 per cent, was described by *The Guardian* newspaper as a 'Euro-slide'. Two-thirds of the voters had endorsed British membership of the Community.

In July 1975, eighteen Labour Members of Parliament took their seats in the European Assembly for the first time and British trade union representatives began to take part in the work of the Economic and Social Committee in Brussels. After fourteen years of hesitation, Britain's membership of the European Economic Community seemed assured for the foreseeable future, though it was not to be the 'full-hearted, whole-hearted and cheerful-hearted support'[4] which *The Guardian* had predicted immediately after the Referendum result. What in the end had persuaded successive British governments of the necessity to join the Community, was a practical, not an idealistic reason; there seemed no satisfactory alternative to membership.

From the European viewpoint, enlargement enormously increased the potential of the Community, in terms of authority and world stature, and of responsibilities and powers. The Community was moving into a new phase, both in terms of its size and of its ambitions. It was also moving beyong the simple political priorities of its early years and into more uncertain areas. The original Community was based on under-standings between the member states worked out for their mutual advantage. The new member states were bound to have different ideas about the Community's priorities and objectives. Challenges were bound to come. The 1970s were already producing radical changes in the political and economic climate of Europe.

4 The Enlarged Community of the 1970s

The climate of the 1970s

The use of the referendum was an innovation in Britain. In other European countries special plebiscites had been used to confirm peaceful alterations to frontiers and changes in sovereignty and the referendum had long been regarded as a useful device for the prevention of constitutional breakdown. But in Britain, with its traditional belief in parliamentary sovereignty, there had been no means of making constitutional changes other than by a majority vote of MPs in Parliament.

The campaign for a referendum on entry into Europe, for the injection of a measure of 'direct democracy' into the British political system, was one of a number of demands for political change which demonstrated that British government, and Parliament in particular, were increasingly felt to be out of touch with British public opinion. Electoral reform for the introduction of proportional representation and the holding of primary elections, and changes in the Committee structure of the House of Commons, were also being canvassed. Other Community countries were facing similar discontent, and were also being forced to re-examine the political structures which they had inherited, in order to meet the needs of new economic and social circumstances.

By the end of the 1960s, technical progress and mass-production had led to increasing prosperity in Western Europe, to which the introduction of the Customs Union and the developing Common Market had contributed considerably. Within the original Community 'three simultaneous revolutions'[1] had been taking place: an agricultural revolution, as the Community moved away from peasant farming towards more capital-intensive agriculture and workers moved out of farming and into industry and the service sectors; a technological revolution of automated processes, with industry organised by large-scale corporations, often multinational, backed by enormous investment and long-term planning; and a structural revolution, as the elimination of tariff and trade barriers between Community member states caused some major sectors of industry and enterprises to shrink and others to expand.

The speed of these changes had upset traditional ways of life and social rhythms. Increasing affluence had led to more education, longer holidays and earlier retirement and individual aspirations were rising and political awareness and expectations increasing. Yet many people were now living in large cities and working in impersonal offices or factories where they felt they could no longer control either their working or living conditions. In France during 1968 popular frustrations boiled over. A violent confrontation in Paris between students and workers and the government was followed by widespread demands for increased political and economic participation. This was the most emphatic demonstration of feelings which were being voiced throughout Europe. Citizens were eager to take a more active part in social and political decision-making, through political parties, local associations and consumer groups. Politics and politicians were having to face the demands of a newly articulate electorate for fuller explanations of and more open debate on government action.

In all the Western democracies, parliamentary government was under criticism. Officials and managers were felt to be too remote from public opinion. The increasingly technical nature of decision-making, over the choice to be made between different types of nuclear power station with their possibly dangerous environmental effects, for example, or over economic forecasting, made it difficult for either parliament or the public to control policy-making.

At the same time, parliaments, governments and political parties, the representative institutions of the political process, were being challenged for power by 'corporate forces', outside the field of government: trade unions, nationalised industries and multinational companies in the industrial field, city and regional administrators at regional level. National governments found themselves having to look for partnership in policy-making with other forces in society which might otherwise block the decision-making process. In order to reach workable agreements – on broad policy objectives, on decisions about priorities and the allocation of limited resources – some sort of consensus had to be reached between the governmental and other, newly influential forces in society.

In Britain, West Germany, the Netherlands and the Scandinavian countries alike, working agreements, or 'social contracts' had been reached between governments, trade unions and employers. These 'social partners' were then consulted on social and economic policy, employment targets, tax changes etc. In return for union restraint on wage increases, and employer restraint on profits and price controls, for example, governments would be committed to social service provisions and to the encouragement of various degrees of 'industrial democracy', often including worker participation in the running of enterprises both at board level and on the shop floor.

In France, the same movement towards national consensus was being achieved by way of planning agreements between government and industry. Throughout Europe, indeed, the movement towards external partnerships, like that of the Economic Community, was being paralleled by moves towards internal power-sharing.

Criticisms of the European Community

If national governments were felt to be increasingly out of touch with the man and woman in the street, it is not surprising that many felt even more out of sympathy with the Brussels 'Eurocrats' in their apparently isolated world. The Commission was described as 'a faceless bureaucracy out for profit'. Its officials were accused, particularly in Britain, of spending much of their working lives in devising unnecessary regulations for the standardisation of Europe's bread and beer, the size of its apples, even the colour of British kippers. Some of these accusations were misunderstandings of over-zealous attempts to set standards for intra-Community trade; often they were sensible and necessary safety measures designed for consumer protection. But they led to disillusionment with the Community's objectives and to a loss of support, in particular from the young and idealistic. The Community was suffering for having concentrated so exclusively on economic and commercial affairs during the 1960s. It had lost what Leo Tindemans was to call its *'parfum d'aventure'*.

Towards the end of the 1960s, the Economic Community began a reappraisal of its achievements and its objectives. The immediate aims of the founding treaties had been achieved, but the signatories were committed to 'an ever closer union among the peoples of Europe', and Community enlargement from six members to nine had brought the Community to a new stage in its development.

A Community summit meeting was held in Paris in October 1972 on the eve of enlargement. It was agreed that the Community should aim at the creation of a new Community, a 'European Union' by 1980, to coincide with the completion of a full Economic and Monetary Union.

The success of the Customs Union and the progress made towards a common market had highlighted the differences arising out of still-existing separate national tax and monetary policies, company law and trade policies. It had shown up the need for more far-reaching common policies in the industrial and economic field. But the new European Union was to go further. Meeting in December 1973, the Heads of State and Government also called for a common approach to foreign policy and outlined a social action programme aimed at providing full and better employment, better living and working conditions and greater citizen participation. Steps to be achieved in 1973 included the setting up of a European Monetary Cooperation Fund and a Regional Development Fund. Leo Tindemans, then Prime Minister of Belgium, was asked to prepare a report on the possible shape of the proposed European Union and on how the Community's institutions might be strengthened to allow for more efficient decision-making and more democratic control.

The Tindemans Report on European Union

Tindemans, an ardent European and a federalist, was also a practical politician. He decided to limit himself to what might be achieved in the present circumstances. His report, compiled after wide consultations, was a series of recommendations for making the existing Community work better and for making Europe more united through extending collective activities. Although he recognised that the Economic and Monetary Union (EMU) would be central to the new Community, and that social, regional and energy policies were also necessary, Tindemans' proposals were essentially political and institutional in nature. EMU was to be placed within a framework of accompanying policies. In his view it was essential that the Community should evolve into a genuine Community 'with a human face', capable of commanding the loyalty of its citizens and strong enough to resist the rival pull of purely national pressures.

He defined a number of different components of a European Union. Institutions would be needed with sufficient power to give political leadership. They must be efficient and capable of taking action where required to ensure equality for all states. Their legitimacy would need to be established by way of democratic control. A European Union would also need to present a united front to the outside world through common action in all the main areas of external relations: foreign policy, economic relations, security and development aid. It would need to have sufficient collective strength to defend its interests and to support law and justice in international discussions.

He felt strongly that the individual states were now dependent upon each other for their economic prosperity. A common economic and monetary policy and common policies in industry and agriculture, energy and research were all therefore necessary to safeguard the future and should logically be treated at European level. The 'solidarity of the peoples of the union' should be ensured, with a regional policy to correct inequalities in development caused by the centralising effect of industrial societies, social action to counteract inequalities of income and encourage a fairer organisation of society. A social policy would be needed to protect the rights and to improve the living standards of the people.

Lastly he emphasised the need for strong political commitment in the member states in order to build such a European Union.

By the time Tindemans presented his report to the Community leaders in 1976 it was obvious that the necessary political commitment, if it had ever existed, had evaporated. European Union was already hopeless except as a distant prospect. Europe was engulfed in economic crisis. Inflation and unemployment were preoccupying the member states. There was little enthusiasm for the new institutional commitments he was proposing. In November 1976 the Heads of State and Government approved the general lines of his recommendations but asked the Community institutions merely to make annual reports to them of progress towards a European Union. The proposals to complete such a union by 1980 were abandoned.

World economic crisis 1973–74

In the early 1970s a major redistribution of the world's wealth began to take place in favour of the oil-producing countries. The Arab-Israeli War of 1973 was followed by a retaliatory steep rise in oil prices by the Arab States and consequently other primary product prices rose too. This was to lead to further inflation, balance-of-payment problems and world monetary disorder. The prospect of a long period of recession and large-scale unemployment faced the industrialised world.

In these circumstances it was not surprising that the Community member state governments should react by trying to control their own economies through independent fiscal measures and steps to deal with unemployment. Each country went its own way in dealing with the oil crisis.* The gap between the strong Community economies and the weaker ones widened; currency crises threatened its existence.

Some of the institutional weaknesses for which the Community was already being criticised and which had worsened since enlargement were now exacerbated by the economic crisis, in particular the complicated nature of its decision-making and its apparent slowness of response to a crisis situation.

Political commitment to integration had declined at a time when the Community was supposed to be moving forward towards a more ambitious phase of integration. Yet the purpose of integration was to help the mixed-economy industrialised democracies of Western Europe, and the political freedom and social equality which they attempt to provide for their citizens, to survive in the modern world. It was essential for the Community to find ways of moving forward in these more difficult circumstances. Tindemans and those whom he had consulted had clearly felt that there was a place for a European level of integration in the new multi-centred pattern of decision-making that was beginning to emerge in the industrialised world. But faced with growing divergences between the economic performance, political circumstances and domestic problems of the member states the Community would now have to prove that it could become an effective regional organisation, at European level, capable of answering at least some of the political problems of the 1970s and 1980s.

The Community was committed by the founding Treaties to 'an ever closer union among the peoples of Europe', but as it moved beyond the Treaties into new, more politically sensitive areas, national interests would be increasingly at issue. Moreover, in the Community of the Nine, the original balance of interests between the member states which had brought the Community into existence was no longer so clear cut. The Community had been built upon unlimited consumption

* See p. 133 for fuller discussion of the 1973–74 oil crisis and the Community's response to it.

and economic growth. It would now have to meet the needs of very different economic circumstances. The influence and the prestige which the Community had already acquired in international affairs would have to be built upon in order to continue to protect the interests of its member states. The Community's newly introduced regional, social and economic policies would need to provide remedies for the continuing unevenness of Europe's economic development.

The introduction of shared institutions above all else had set the Community apart from other intergovernmental organisations. Designed for the achievement of a Common Market in the prosperous 1960s, they would now have to provide both the stability and the necessary adaptability for integrated policy-making in the future. They would need to offer a protective and efficient framework, without at the same time restricting the Community's further development. To many observers European integration was already furthest advanced in the field of law. For the Treaty of Rome and the other Community treaties had provided for the establishment of a European Court and for the provision of a common legal system between the members, which went far beyond any previous legal arrangements made between independent states.

5 A New Legal Order

Community law is both international and municipal, public and private, enacted and formulated in precedents. It is *sui generis* law and must be treated as such.[1]

In 1976, three years after Britain had joined the European Community, a London magistrate recommended that a Frenchman, who worked in London, should be deported after his conviction for possessing cannabis. The recommendation was challenged, on the grounds that it would infringe the right of freedom of movement for workers within the European Community, laid down by the Treaty of Rome. In another instance, a court trying a case of smuggling was faced with the argument that the offence should not exist at all, and that its continuance on the statute book contravened EEC customs laws.

Both cases illustrate the fact that a new element has entered the legal systems of the EEC member states. European Community law is a system of laws which, in certain areas, is directly applicable to persons and institutions in the member states and which can be invoked by citizens in their national courts.

Before the founding of the Community, courts operating beyond national boundaries had been set up by international agreement. The International Court of Justice at the Hague, for example, acts as the judiciary of the United Nations, hears cases and gives judgment in disputes between member states and can advise and give opinions to the organs of the United Nations itself. The Court of Human Rights at Strasbourg, founded by the Council of Europe, can give judgments in favour of individuals and against those states which recognise its right to judge. Similar functions are also performed by the Court of Justice of the Community. This Court also supervises Community law. The Community too, although it is not itself a state, has in certain specified areas acquired power to legislate and to make legal decisions and to have them carried out. The Treaties granted certain powers to the Community institutions and in so doing gave them authority to bind the member states, also their citizens, individually.

Community law is limited in its application to specific areas laid down by the Treaties. In many fields national law is still supreme, for example, in most areas of criminal law and domestic civil law, but in others, Community law already touches on many aspects of national life. For example, banking, insurance, taxation, company law, the law governing monopolies and restrictive practices, patent and trade-marks, private international law and law of the sea have all been con-siderably affected. In areas such as immigration, control of foreign workers, matters relating to equality between the sexes, consumer and environmental protection on which the Treaty of Rome gives guidelines, national law has been challenged, or influenced. All this represents a loss of legal sovereignty by the member states. By joining the Community, they surrendered far-reaching powers to a new and independent legal order, which can act in Community affairs on the international scene and which can bind its members.

Sources of Community law

The three European founding Treaties are the primary source of Com-munity law, laying down the principles and rules which are binding on all Community members, since the nature of the Community itself, its existence, and its functioning, demand a consistent application of Community law between the member states. The *acts* of the Commun-ity represent a second source of Community law. Where uniform rules are needed, it can legislate directly, through *regulations* which are binding in law throughout the Community. They are automatically incorporated into the national legal systems of member states without specific individual ratification.

Where uniformity is not essential, the Community can work through the legal systems of the member states. In such cases, the Commission can use *directives*, which indicate a broad objective and call on the member states to which they are addressed to implement these objec-tives in their own way. Directives require some legal action, which normally amounts to legislation, by the member states before they become national law. *Decisions* of the Commission are directed specifically to an individual or an enterprise, and are also binding on them. *Recommendations* and *opinions* given by the Council of Ministers or the Commission on matters of general or particular concern do not have the force of law, but are useful since they can test the reaction to a proposed new policy without formally committing the Commission to that action.

The European Court

The Treaties declare that the Community's legal system applies throughout the Community and must not be impeded. The European Court of Justice, which sits in Luxembourg, ensures that Community law is observed in the interpretation and application of the Treaties. Its judgments bind member states and institutions. It also interprets the law and may leave its application to national jurisdictions, so that the national courts also participate in the legal development of the Community and in the application of Community law on the national scene.

The Court reviews the lawfulness of the acts of the Council, of the Commission, of the member state governments and in certain areas, of citizens, in respect of their Community obligations. The validity of a Community regulation or directive may be appealed to the Court and if such an appeal is upheld, the Community regulation or directive in question may be declared null and void. Appeals against acts or omissions by any of the institutions or member state governments can be lodged by any other institution or government, by firms, and, notably, by individual citizens who are directly affected by the nature of the matter.

The ten judges* of the European Court are appointed by member state governments for a six-year period. The Court is assisted by one of four Advocates-General, who does not act on behalf of any of the parties to the dispute, or of the Community, but as an *amicus curiae*, in the nature of an independent judicial observer who represents the public interest. The judges reach their decisions by majority vote and present them in open court. The Court's judgments are directly applicable in the member states and are enforceable through the national courts. It can make orders concerning costs and can grant legal aid.

The precedence of Community over national law

The transfer to the Community of sovereign rights over certain legal,

---

* On 1 January 1981 Greece formally joined the EEC to become the Community's tenth member state. See p. 129.

administrative and judicial powers formed one of the major objections to Community membership voiced in the United Kingdom at the time of the Referendum campaign. That this transfer took place is now accepted. It follows that Community citizens are affected by two legal systems, a national and the Community system. Courts of law must apply both systems of law where they are relevant, and where there is a conflict, the Community law takes precedence. This was originally established in some of the member states by specific national constitutional provision; the Dutch constitution, for example, specifically enacted the supremacy of Community over national law. In the United Kingdom, the precedence of Community law is recognised by the European Communities Act, through its acceptance of the jurisprudence of the European Court. The supremacy of Community law is also implicit in the nature of the Communities themselves, since their existence and functioning requires the application of that law. This has been reinforced by a number of judgments of the Community Court which ensure that the surrender of sovereignty cannot subsequently be reversed by any measure taken by national authorities which is in conflict with the Community concept.[2]

The political role of Community law

The Community legal system has often been compared with that of the federal system of the United States. The basic document of the law, the Constitution, was drafted in terms of general intention and the Supreme Court was left to interpret it and to give it practical meaning. By the process of judicial review, over Congressional measures and over state laws, the law in the United States has become an instrument in fulfilling the original intentions of the Constitution. The European Community is also a political structure which emerged out of a general act of will; it is an independent structure set up by a number of states which at that time were looking for something separate from and superior to the nation state. It too depends heavily on statements of general principle and about broad objectives. The United States Supreme Court plays a partly political role, the upholding of federal aims. A comparable role is also fulfilled by the legal system of the European Community, whose law has been described as the 'motor' to enable it to move towards its ultimate aim, the 'ever closer union' referred to in the preamble of the Treaty of Rome.

The existence of the Court as arbiter on questions of interpretation of Community law has strengthened the Community as a political system. Defiance of its rulings by member states has been exceptional.[3] Where the Commission may not feel able to challenge a member state directly on a matter which raises sensitive political issues, it can refer breaches of Community law to the European Court. The Court can also pioneer political advance in the way in which it interprets the Community Treaties to foster the cohesiveness of the Community.

By creating a body of independent Community law, by upholding the authority of the institutions, by exercising its powers to influence the resolution of conflicts between the member states, by asserting federal prerogatives, the European Court interprets the Treaties in such a way as to promote the survival of the Community.

Harmonisation of laws

The evolution of Community law in its pursuit of the Treaty objectives also has the effect of harmonising the laws of the member states, principally in the economic field but also in wider areas.

The national courts are responsible for aligning national case law with Community law and with each other's laws and indeed, in certain areas, for example those concerned with customs duties, the movement of workers, the mutual recognition of qualifications, taxation and export aids, the Treaty of Rome contains clear directions. In the field of competition, the Commission has special powers in curbing restrictions in trade between member states so as to promote the proper functioning of a Community-wide market. Provision is also being made for the recognition of European patents, for Community laws to protect the environment and for a European Company Statute.

Legal styles

A complication which has affected British lawyers since the United Kingdom joined the Community, has been that the Continental system of public administration and constitutional law is very different from traditional English common law, a system based on judge-made law and on precedent. Continental legal systems have been more emphatically based on written constitutions and on comprehensive codes of law. This difference has contributed also to differences in traditional legal reasoning and approach and is now influencing British lawyers to adopt new techniques. The Treaty of Rome is also a comprehensive code of law which, often only in outline, sets out the rights and duties of governments and individuals, from which rights and remedies can be deduced. Ministers and civil servants are more often concerned with such broadly stated law than was previously the case in Britain, in formulating policy and rules.

West Germany, France and Italy all felt a need to reinforce the powers of their respective national governments after the war, by spelling out precise rights and duties to demand obedience. In these countries, the body of constitutional law has been more important than in Britain, where sovereignty has traditionally rested more firmly in Parliament. It is noteworthy that membership of the European Community now creates possibilities of appeal to the European Court against an Act òf Parliament which is in conflict with the Treaty of Rome.

In Community law, the intentions of the legislators are all-important. The laws are part of a larger design which will continue to develop. To the European Court, Community aims may count more than a literal construction of legal texts, whereas in Britain, judges have in the past often been concerned with the precise meaning of words, the letter of the law, rather than the more general intentions. While some recent laws in Britain are intended to establish standards of behaviour which were previously not widely adopted, such as the Race Relations Act of 1965 and the Industrial Relations Act of 1971, English law has traditionally been more concerned with enacting practices already more generally accepted.[4]

The legal character of the Community is apparent in all its institutions, which are all concerned with influencing, shaping and controlling the legislative output of the Community. Under the founding Treaties, for example, the Commission was made the Community 'watchdog', with the job of seeing that the Treaties are observed. It is also the institution which both originates and administers the Community laws.

6 The Roles of the Commission and of the Council

The Commission of the European Communities, established in its Brussels headquarters, the vast Berlaymont building, its staff over-flowing into office blocks in neighbouring streets of the Schuman Quarter, has often been associated, particularly by the British press, with bureaucratic excesses. Even today this reputation is not wholly merited and in the Community's early days, particularly under the Presidency of Walter Hallstein, between 1958 and 1967, the Commission was compared by some to a band of partisans, fighting for the European cause, and was admired for its energy, understanding, creativity and strong *esprit de corps*.

When Jean Monnet first led the French delegation into the long meetings which preceded the founding of the European Coal and Steel Community in 1952, the other delegations were delighted to find that he did not adopt inflexible negotiating positions but invited them to discuss and to contribute to the finding of common solutions to what were regarded as common problems. His approach helped to convert a number of tough national negotiators into committed Europeans, some of whom eventually went to Luxembourg to work on the staff of the new High Authority, and later, of the EEC Commission, which inherited this strong commitment to European unity.[1] But over the years its initial enthusiasm has diminished, as the Commission has failed to develop in the ways envisaged by the Community's founders. This is partly a reflection of a general loss of commitment to action at Community level and it is also due to the fact that the various roles which the Commission was given to play have been too diverse and too contradictory.

There are at present fourteen Commissioners, each chosen by joint agreement between the governments of the member states, two from each of the larger countries, France, Britain, West Germany and Italy; one from Denmark, Greece, Ireland and each of the Benelux coun-

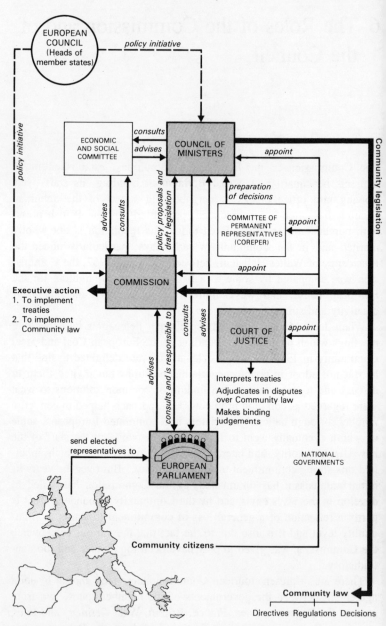

The institutions of the Community

tries. A President is chosen by agreement between the member states from among the fourteen, serving for a two-year term of office which is renewable. Once appointed, the Commission members take an oath before the Court of Justice in Luxembourg. They undertake that for the four years of their appointment they will not seek to represent national interests, but will try to move the Community forward towards its stated aims of further integration. There are, however, continuous informal contacts between the Commissioners and their national capitals, through the personal 'cabinets', or higher secretariats, of each Commissioner.

The Commission is responsible to the European Parliament, which, by a vote of censure passed by a two-thirds majority, could force all the Commissioners collectively to resign. Individual Commissioners, however, are not accountable to and cannot be dismissed by the Parliament. Nor can Commissioners be dismissed by the member state governments during their terms of office.

The Commission meets at least weekly, to discuss an agenda prepared by its secretariat. It is served by a staff which is comparable in size with one of the smaller British Government Departments, for example, the Scottish Office. They work in a number of services which include a statistical office and legal service and twenty Directorates-General which control a multitude of functions including external relations, agriculture, social affairs, energy and transport. Each member of the Commission is responsible for one or more of these main areas of Community acitivity.[2]

As guardian of the Treaties, the Commission is responsible for taking to the European Court anyone, individual, enterprise or government, which does not conform to the Treaties, or to regulations or decisions subsequently made by the institutions under the Treaties. If there is a breach of the Community rules, for example of the agricultural regulations, or of import controls, the Commission must investigate, issue a ruling or decision and notify the parties concerned of the action to be taken.

The Commission acts as the Community's diplomatic representative on all matters on which it has been mandated by the Council of Ministers. It is also the executive arm of the Community, responsible for implementing Community legislation. Its executive powers arise from two sources: firstly from the Treaties, and secondly from 'derived' Community law, resulting from Council decisions which give the

Commission extra responsibilities for management and administration.

The Commission's administrative duties

The Commission administers Community funds, for example the levies on coal and steel producers which under the ECSC Treaty are used to retrain redundant workers, and for modernisation schemes. It administers the European Social Fund, the European Development Fund which provides financial and technical cooperation for developing countries, and the Agricultural Guidance and Guarantee Fund for market support and farm modernisation schemes.

It carries out settled policies, in relation to the Coal and Steel Treaty provisions, the Customs Union, the Common External Tariff and the Common Agricultural Policy. The Commission was given direct powers by the Treaties with regard to Competition policy. Its duties include the investigation of restrictive agreements and of abuses of dominant trading positions of a kind prohibited by the ECSC and Rome Treaties. In this area, the Commission can prosecute or warn individuals and enterprises for breaches of the Treaty rules.

Commissioners attend meetings of the permanent committees and plenary sessions of the European Parliament when matters within their spheres are discussed and must be ready to defend or justify their own proposals. They must be present at question-time to answer oral questions on Community affairs from Members of Parliament.

The Commission's right to initiate Community policy

The Commission's most complex roles are those of initiator of Community policy and of advocate of the Community interest in the Council of Ministers.

Community proposals and legislation, whether in the form of regulations, directives, recommendations or opinions, originate in draft proposals from the Commission. Each proposal may take months or even years to emerge in its final form, since at every stage in its preparation Commission staff consult widely, with national civil servants, employers' organisations, trade unions and other interested groups, in the course of the thorough research which may be required. A number of advisory committees made up of the heads of representative bodies for particular sectors, for example financial and economic affairs, agricultural production, or social welfare, will meet to discuss the proposals in question.

Once a proposal has been formulated and presented to the Council of Ministers in draft form, the Commission's representatives will attend meetings of the Council's committees and of the Council itself and will help the Council to reach a decision, but representing the general rather than national interests, seeking compromise solutions, but always with an eye to the maximum Community advantage. For the Commission is also committed to acting as the 'conscience' of the Community, responsible for reminding it of its fundamental objectives, suggesting new paths for it to follow, and pressing for further integration. The President of the Commission is expected to play an important part in giving an intellectual lead to integration, by putting forward proposals intended to influence the broader directions of Community progress. Roy Jenkins was acting in this way, for example, when late in 1977 he made a major speech in Florence in which he revived the proposal for a European Monetary Union, which he saw as an essential step to be taken if the Community was to move forward towards further integration.

The dilemma of the Commission
One of the elements in the Community crisis of 1965 was de Gaulle's challenge to the right of the Commission to initiate policy. The outcome of that crisis was to confirm this right of initiative, but in future the Commission was to consult more closely with member state governments and to act less independently. With the lessening of enthusiasm in the larger member states for the political unification of Europe, the Commission has found it increasingly difficult to achieve its broader objectives. Many of its proposals have been rejected by the Council of Ministers. Its policies have consequently become less ambitious and more deferential to the wishes of national governments. Many of its schemes die through lack of political support.

Over twenty years after the inauguration of the Community many of its Directorates-General have not yet got comprehensive common policies to work on. This is particularly so in areas where national interests and influences are strong. Although a common transport policy was one of the three policies, together with agriculture and external commerce, specifically mentioned in the Treaty of Rome, no comprehensive policy has been agreed upon. The transport industry absorbs 10 per cent of national incomes and 10 per cent of the Community's work force. It appears to be for political reasons that the

Community's present transport policy is limited to a programme of harmonisation covering such matters as vehicle weights and dimensions, drivers' hours and working conditions, rather than forming an integrated policy. Most of the larger issues which it would seem sensible to tackle at Community level, such as the relationship between different forms of transport, road and rail, public or private, the effects of transport planning on the environment and the likely effects of energy shortages, have yet to be tackled.

The Commission's independence of the national governments and its ability to hold and follow a consistent view of Community objectives, interpreted in the light of changing conditions, are important ingredients in what distinguishes the Community from other intergovernmental international organisations. But while the national governments of the larger member states are no longer committed to political unification, the Commission needs to be able to lobby for and to publicise its own objectives.

In a national government, it is the Cabinet which initiates policy and the Cabinet is responsible to and derives its authority from an elected assembly. The Commission is appointed, not elected and has no political base. Yet in its role of moving the Community forward it needs to use political pressure.

If the Community is to extend its scope, towards an Economic and Monetary Union for example, then it must become more answerable to public opinion and to Parliament. One suggestion for giving the Commission political authority has been through the election of its President. Community supporters have always hoped that the Commission would gain some political support from and become increasingly responsible to the directly elected European Parliament, with individual Commissioners subject to dismissal by the Parliament, which would also have a say in their appointment. Parliaments after all exist to support as well as to control ministers and governments.

The bureaucratisation of the Commission

As national positions have become increasingly entrenched, the Commission has had to spend more of its time in trying to get agreement in the Council of Ministers and often in the process it has had to compromise its broader vision of Community progress for the sake of a small gain. While so many of its policy initiatives are blocked by the Council of Ministers, it is not surprising that the Commission should have tended to concentrate upon its other bureaucratic, administrative role. This has grown rapidly as the Community itself has become bigger and more complex. Its critics now complain that the Commission spends too much time on bureaucratic detail and not enough on long-term planning.

The Commission has looked for ways of helping it to deal with the burdens of administration. Management committees were introduced into the agricultural system, for example. There is one for each main agricultural market and members are national government representatives who sit with the Commission to monitor its proposals. Their main duty is to harmonise Community and national points of view. If a management committee agrees with the Commission proposal, it can go into force; if not, there is an appeal procedure to the Council of Ministers. Such committees can prevent deadlock in decision-making and their use has gradually been extended, for example to the procedures for setting Community-wide technical and health standards.

Management committees have introduced more national administrators into the Community process, in itself an important step towards Community acceptance, but their members are not necessarily committed Europeans. Nowadays too the Commission is staffed according to a national quota system. Its top jobs are in practice in the gift of national governments and are allocated on a national basis. As a result, promotion prospects depend not only upon ability, but upon nationality. Since promotion prospects in general are poor, staff trade unions insist upon job security. Except in rare circumstances Eurocrats can neither be dismissed, nor moved to other jobs without their consent. Some critics, including Ralf Dahrendorf, the West German sociologist and former Commissioner of the European Communities, currently Director of the London School of Economics, have said that they would prefer to see the appointment of Ministers for Europe, or the strengthening of the Presidency of the Council of Ministers as ways of increasing the Community's political answerability, rather than risk strengthening the increasingly bureaucratic Commission.

The Commission has kept and continues to keep the Community working and to produce proposals for long-term Community progress. For the moment, the direction of Community development has been tilted towards intergovernmental procedures, with no immediate likelihood of the original independent and autonomous functions of the Commission increasing. The relationship between the Commission and the Council of Ministers has been described as a dialogue. At present it is a dialogue in which the Council has very much the last word. However, a number of organisations have developed which act as mediating bodies between the Commission and the Council and which span both the European and the national outlooks. These have developed out of the Council of Ministers.

The Council of Ministers

As the power of the Commission has declined, so the part played in Community decision-making by the Council of Ministers, an entirely intergovernmental body, has increased. It has been described as 'the sole effective centre of power in the Community system',[3] for it is within the Council of Ministers that the vote is taken which turns Commission proposals into Community law.

Each member government sends one of its ministers to the meetings of the Council of Ministers. The Council of Foreign Ministers and the Financial Council meet more frequently than most of the others. There are Agricultural, Transport, and Industrial Councils which are convened according to the subject under discussion. The Presidency of the Council is held for six months by each member state in turn. Meetings are prepared beforehand in the national capitals, where negotiating positions are decided upon and ministers and national officials are briefed. In Brussels, a Council Secretariat composed of officials from all the member states works in the Charlemagne building.

When the Council receives a legislative proposal from the Commission it is sent out to the European Parliament for an opinion. Once received back by the Council it will be looked at by the Committee of Permanent Representatives (COREPER) and sent to one of the Council's special committees of senior officials for detailed study. All important questions and those with political implications are discussed by the full Council. The Commission is represented at all meetings of Council working parties and committees; its representatives attend, but do not vote in Council meetings. Their task is to work for acceptance of Commission proposals by the member states, so that Community legislation can be enacted, even if eventually in watered-down form.

Council meetings involve long intergovernmental bargaining. Concessions often take the form of 'package deals' which offer some advantage to each member state. Acceptable settlements may not be reached until after apparent deadlock, only resolved after 'marathon' night-long meetings. Once a proposal is adopted, the ministers concerned may have to convince their home administrations that they have made the best deal possible. The European Parliament and other advocates of more open government would like these meetings to be held in public, with publication of the proceedings.

Voting in the Council

Voting within the Council, as specified by the Treaties, may be by unanimous vote, or by absolute or qualified majority. In a vote by absolute majority, each member state has one vote and a simple majority decision is binding. A qualified majority is determined by giving each member state a specified number of votes: ten to each of the four largest states, the United Kingdom, France, West Germany and Italy; five each to Belgium, Greece and the Netherlands; three to Denmark and Ireland, and two to Luxembourg. Forty-five votes out of the total of sixty-three constitute a majority.

Most measures considered decisive for Community progress, for example those relating to harmonisation of legislation have always required unanimous decisions of the Council. In January 1966, majority voting in certain other areas was due to come into force automatically under the founding Treaties. This prospect had helped to spark off the constitutional crisis in the Community of the previous months. The 'Luxembourg compromise' eventually accepted that in the then current climate within the Community it would be unreasonable to impose majority voting where important national issues were at stake.

To avoid the destructive use of the veto which the unanimous vote gives to the member state governments, the usual practice is to postpone a decision when one country objects to a proposal, or to reserve the right to veto it, in order to get changes made to it. Governments do not apply the Treaty provisions for majority voting, except in relation to the budget and to decisions of the Agricultural Management Committees, where action is needed within a fixed time. The result has been to slow down decision-making in the Community, with Commission proposals and even decisions by Heads of State and Government, blocked in the Council of Ministers. Critics would like to see unanimous voting reserved for essential matters only.

Committees of the Council

Because of the growing amount of work involved, a number of

specialised committees were set up which report directly to the Council. In 1958, a Monetary Committee was formed which consisted of officials from Ministries of Finance and of the central banks in the member states, together with Commission officials. It prepares ministerial meetings on economic and monetary cooperation and keeps the monetary and financial situation of the member states under review. A number of economic committees have been founded to try to find common approaches to international monetary problems. They include the Short-term, and Medium-term Economic Committees, the Budgetary Policy Committee and, in 1974, the Committee of Central Bank Governors.

Other Council Committees and working groups, established since 1966, include the Transport Committee, the Special Committee on Agriculture and, in 1970, the Standing Committee on Employment, chaired by the President of the Council and made up of representatives of employers' organisations, the trade unions and the Commission. Most important of all in this growing network of Committees is the Committee of Permanent Representatives (Comité des Représentants Permanents).

The Committee of Permanent Representatives (COREPER)

Each member state has a Permanent Representation to the European Communities in Brussels, headed by an Ambassador or Permanent Representative, with a staff of diplomats and officials seconded from the national civil service, to assist him. The Treaty of Rome set up a Committee of these Permanent Representatives, which was intended to liaise between the national administrations and the Community institutions, to explain Community activities to national governments, to transmit information and documents, and to supply expert advice to Council Committees. One of the effects of the 1966 Community agreements was to give a more important role to this Committee, moreover the Brussels Treaty, by which the institutions of the three original Communities were merged from the beginning of 1967, recognised the Committee as an official Community institution.

Most Commission proposals[4] now go to COREPER before going to the Council and are discussed first by it or by one if its subcommittees. It can make decisions on certain issues on which there is known to be national agreement, matters such as the harmonisation of standards, or export credit guidelines or the free movement of nurses, or lawyers, throughout the Community. These measures are then automatically adopted by the Council. Issues over which there is disagreement go on to the agenda for Council discussion.

Although there were Commission fears that COREPER's growing influence might damage the Commission's authority and rights of initiative, in practice COREPER has acted as a 'hinge' between the Commission and the Council of Ministers, in many cases supporting a Community line against that of the national governments. Many of its staff are appointed to Brussels on a long-term basis; they know and understand each other's outlook and particular problems. COREPER *Groupes de Travail* meet weekly with Commission officials, and regular meetings take place between the Commission President and the Chairman of COREPER. Some of the inter-state bargaining which once had to be negotiated by the Commission, now takes place in COREPER meetings. Its development has helped to reduce the bottleneck of decision-making at Council level.

In October 1973, however, the oil supply crisis again demonstrated that the Community could not react with sufficient speed and unanimity when world events required it. It was followed by growing divergences between the economies of the member states which presented a real threat to Community unity. New measures of 'crisis management' were needed. Decisions would have to be taken at the very top of the governmental structure to be effective.

Foreign policy coordination: the European Council and political cooperation
In order to prevent the institutions from being dominated by the national governments, the Heads of State and Government in the member countries were originally given very little part to play in Community affairs, apart from being called together when amendments to the Treaties themselves were necessary. After the 1963 Treaty between France and Germany, the Heads of State and Government of those two countries began to meet at frequent intervals.

Throughout the 1960s, at de Gaulle's insistence, political cooperation and economic integration were kept well apart. The Community was only competent to deal with the 'low' policy areas of economic and social affairs; the national governments alone were considered competent to deal with 'high' policy political issues, a distinction which became increasingly blurred as the Community extended its sphere of activities. At the Hague Conference in 1969, it was agreed to hold regular 'Summit' meetings of the Heads of State and Government as an opportunity for high-level planning of the Community's future. A Committee was set up under Viscount Davignon, then the Belgian Foreign Minister, subsequently a Community Commissioner, to look into the possibilities of a common foreign policy.

At Paris in December 1974, the Heads of Government agreed 'gradually to adopt common positions and coordinate their diplomatic action in all areas of international affairs which affect the interests of the European Community'. 'Summit' meetings of the Heads of State and Government were to be known in future as the European Council, and were to be held regularly three times a year and whenever 'crisis management' required it.

The European Council is the only body to have some jurisdiction in all fields. Foreign policy and defence can be discussed together with matters such as regional and employment policy which are within the competence of the Community. Although it exists outside the official Community institutions, it is both an initiating and decision-making body. It now sets the pace for policy-making in the Community and the Council of Ministers takes fewer decisions when a European Council meeting is imminent. 'Summits' have been criticised for concentrating on crisis issues and neglecting other matters, but they have become established as a recognised channel for conducting European affairs.

The ten foreign ministers also meet regularly as part of the political cooperation procedures, quite apart from their meetings as the Community's Council of Foreign Ministers and a Political Committee composed in most cases of the head of the Political Directorate of each Foreign Ministry meets at least monthly. (In most member states, the Foreign Ministers, unlike the British Foreign Office, are divided into Political, Economic and Administrative Directorates; the British Foreign Office is usually represented in the Political Committee by a deputy Permanent Under-Secretary.) It appoints working groups of experts to study both wide policy areas, such as the Middle East and the Mediterranean, and also particular issues, for example European security. A *Groupe de Correspondants*, European experts from each foreign ministry, meets before and after Political Committee meetings and a special telex system, known as *Coreu*, links the Foreign Ministries and is coordinated by the Foreign Ministry of the country holding the Presidency of the Council of Ministers.

Community ambassadors also play their part in the political cooperation network. Community ambassadors at the United Nations meet twice-weekly to coordinate policies and the country holding the Presidency of the Council of Ministers often speaks on behalf of the Ten in the UN Assembly. Community embassies brief each other after official visits to or from third countries. Joint consultation and preparation, such as that which took place before the Belgrade Conference on European Security in 1977, enable the Community to establish a common position in international negotiations. COREPER, though not involved directly, may become drawn in through the repercussions of political cooperation decisions on Community policies. The decision to impose Community sanctions on Iran in 1980, for example, clearly had such repercussions.

At first both the Commission and the European Parliament viewed the introduction of intergovernmental political cooperation procedures with misgivings. But since the late 1970s, the Commission has taken part in all ministerial meetings and is represented at meetings of the Political Committee and of its working groups. The European Parliament too has developed procedural links with the political cooperation network.

Foreign policy coordination lies outside the Treaty framework. The new procedures which have no formal recognition were intended to streamline decision-making, to coordinate national policies and to give *grandes orientations* to future political cooperation. They were an attempt to create an effective and flexible method of cooperation at all levels, and activities within their framework are increasing rapidly. However, each country is ultimately responsible for its own foreign policy. As Chapter 11 will show, there is no common Community foreign policy.

The nation states remain the most powerful political realities of Europe in the late twentieth century, but procedures for political cooperation could prove to be the first steps towards closer union. Even staunch federalists, such as Jean Monnet, recognised that since any kind of political integration seemed premature, some form of political cooperation would be a way in which consultation and coordination of policies could take place and decision-making in emergencies be speeded up.

In the late 1970s, the Commission was still fully occupied with its bureaucratic functions and was lacking in representative authority. The member states were increasingly lukewarm towards integration and were absorbed by national preoccupations. So supporters of further integration turned to the European Parliament, now directly elected by universal suffrage, for hopes of progress.

7 The European Parliament and Democratic Accountability

In the European Coal and Steel Community, a Common Assembly was given extensive supervisory powers over the High Authority. The Treaty of Rome created a new assembly, later to be known as the European Parliament, for the Economic Community. It was originally an assembly of delegates, nominated from among the members of the national parliaments, but according to the Treaty, it was eventually to be elected by direct universal suffrage, with gradually increasing powers. No firm date was given by which these changes were to be made, and for over twenty years, the limited powers and delegated membership of the Assembly were a reminder that the crucial element of democratic legitimacy was still missing from the Community.

Towards the end of the 1960s, as the Economic Community lost impetus and strong criticisms of the Community's institutional structure were being voiced, strengthening the European parliament was seen as one way of counteracting an increasingly bureaucratic Commission and the secrecy of procedures and national rivalries within the Council of Ministers. The Vedel Committee was set up by the Commission to examine the future of the European Parliament. It proposed the implementation of the original intention of direct elections, and a gradual increase in the Parliament's legislative functions.

Not all the member state governments were prepared to surrender further control to an assembly with increasingly independent authority. Both Britain and France were emphatic in their opposition, and for a time it began to look as though the introduction of a directly elected assembly might be delayed indefinitely by disagreements over increasing the powers of that parliament. It was finally decided, at the Paris Summit meeting in 1974, to go ahead with proposals for direct elections, on the understanding that they would entail no formal increase in the new Parliament's powers. A 1977 British Government White Paper again emphasised that government support for the elections was conditional upon the powers of the Assembly remaining as they were, while in France, the law providing for the elections was passed only after a ruling by the French Constitutional Court that no increased powers were involved. Committed Europeans nevertheless always hoped that even if proposals requiring Treaty amendments proved unacceptable, the existing powers of the Parliament could be stretched, and that direct elections would inevitably give it more authority.

The first European Parliament to be elected by direct universal suffrage began its five-year term of office in July 1979. Its 410 seats, more than double the number in the nominated assembly it replaced, were allocated so that France, West Germany, Italy and the United Kingdom received 81 seats each, the Netherlands 25, Belgium 24, Denmark 16, Ireland 15 and Luxembourg 6. Greek members are at present nominated from among the members of the Athens parliament. When she joined the Community in 1981 Greece was allocated 24 seats, and Portugal will receive the same number if, as seems likely, she joins the Community during the 1980s. The entry of Spain, with an expected allocation of 58 seats, would bring the total for the Parliament of twelve member states to 516.

The European Parliament holds some of its monthly sessions in Strasbourg, its official home, and some in Luxembourg, its administrative and secretarial headquarters. Each month files, documents and staff move back and forth between the two cities, an expensive and time-consuming reminder of the need to demonstrate that one country cannot be allowed to dominate the Community and its institutions.*

A President and eleven Vice-presidents are elected annually from among the members and together with the leaders of the party political groups form a Parliamentary Bureau. This is responsible for the administration and organisation of the Parliament's work and for the appointment of the Secretary-General, whose job is similar to that of the Clerk to the House of Commons at Westminster. The Chairmen and Rapporteurs of each of Parliament's fifteen permanent, specialised committees are nominated by the political groups.

---

* Although in July 1981 the European Parliament voted to hold all future full sessions in Strasbourg, the issue is by no means settled.

Political groups in the European Parliament

So far candidates for election to the European Parliament have stood as representatives of their national parties and not as members of European political groups; but within the 'hemicycle', the horse-shoe-shaped chamber in which Parliament meets, members sit according to European political groupings.

In the Parliament which began its five-year life in 1979 there are six main groups and twenty independent members. Socialists form the largest single group, as they did in the previous delegated Parliament, with 120 out of the 434 seats and members from each of the Community countries (see Table 7.1 below). Eleven of the independent members, including a group of Danish anti-marketeers have formed the Group for the Technical Coordination and Defence of Independent Groups and members. Nine members, among them Ian Paisley, the Democratic Unionist member for Ulster are unattached.

Table 7.1 *Political groups in the European Parliament, 1981*

	B	DK	F	G*	I	IRL	L	NL	UK	WG	Total
Socialists	7	4	22	7	13	4	1	9	18	35	120
European People's Party (CD)	10	–	8	–	30	4	3	10	–	42	107
European Democrats	–	3	–	–	–	–	–	–	61	–	64
Communists	–	1	19	1	24	–	–	–	–	–	45
Liberals	4	3	17	–	5	1	2	4	–	4	40
European Progressive Democrats	–	1	15	–	–	5	–	–	1	–	22
Group for the Technical Coordination and Defence of Independent Groups and Members	1	4	–	–	5	1	–	–	–	–	11
Non-attached	2	–	–	–	4	–	–	2	1	–	9
Total	24	16	81	24	81	15	6	25	81	81	*434*

* Since 1 January 1981 24 Greek members have joined the European Parliament. Pending elections in Greece they have been nominated by their various parties and, therefore, hold a dual mandate. The 16 New Democracy Party members have not yet joined a political group in the European Parliament.

Each group has its own staff and secretariat. Within the group, debate tends to be livelier than it is on the floor of the house, where speeches are prepared beforehand and the proceedings slowed down by simultaneous translation into all the Community languages. Attempts are made to reach common positions within the political group before the full sessions of the house. The Socialist Group, for example, meets for three days prior to a plenary session of the Parliament to discuss reports and papers. Group discipline is weaker than in most national parties and there are no sanctions against members who vote against an agreed position. The European Democrats, who are mainly drawn from the British Conservative party, have attempted to reproduce the Westminster whipping system and have appointed a Chief Whip, assisted by Junior Whips; although the system has been tightened up since direct elections it still does not have the force of the Westminster system. A three-line whip would be issued on matters involving agriculture or the Community budget, but on both issues Danish members might disagree with their British colleagues and no sanctions would be applied to them. In all the groups the group secretariats form the link between the Parliamentary group and the wider European party federations.

The powers of the Parliament

In most western democracies national parliaments expect to enjoy certain, often hard-won, powers. They include the right to exercise some control over financial affairs and the appointment and dismissal of the governing executive, together with some control over the enactment of laws. But the legislative powers of parliaments in modern states are increasingly subject to restraints. Governments, not parliaments, propose most new legislation. In the United Kingdom, for example, the opportunities for Members of Parliament to present Private Members Bills are very limited. Nor is it possible to draw direct parallels between the functioning of the Community's institutions and the national ones. Community institutions do not constitute a government in the national sense and the European Parliament does not have to sustain an executive, nor is it elected to carry out a comprehensive political programme. The areas of decision-making which are within the Community's competence at present are firmly circumscribed and the decision-making which it can exercise, save in specific areas, such as agriculture and competition, lies with the Council of Ministers alone.

The Community's Parliament is not primarily intended to be a legislative body, but a consultative one. Its job is to represent the views of the electorate on issues which come within the Community's competence. It is also expected to act as an *organisme de contrôle*, exercising supervisory powers over the decision-making bodies; both Commission proposals and Council decisions are influenced by Parliament's opinions.

All draft Bills are sent to Parliament for an opinion before being discussed in the Council of Ministers. They are first examined by one of Parliament's fifteen permanent committees, which between them cover the major aspects of Community business. Committee membership broadly reflects the political composition of the Parliament as a whole. Members are appointed for the five-year life of the Parliament and meet not in Strasbourg or in Luxembourg, but in Brussels, where they can more easily call on representatives of the Commission and make requests to the Council of Ministers, to give evidence and answer questions on the proposals under examination. It is in the standing Committees that the bulk of the Parliament's work is carried out and in the course of five years, many members become experts on the subjects they cover. The scope and expertise of the permanent committees has impressed even some anti-European British members of the European Parliament.

After thorough examination in Committee, the draft legislation will be reported on by the Committee's rapporteur to a full session of Parliament, again with Commission representatives and Council members present to answer questions. Parliament can either accept the proposal by giving a favourable opinion on it, or send it back to the Commission with suggested amendments. In 1978, Parliament amended 49 out of the 175 Commission proposals it received. All or part of 32 amendments were accepted by the Commission. In certain circumstances proposals can originate in the European Parliament itself, by means of resolutions requesting other Community institutions, notably the Commission, to take appropriate actions.

In addition to its advisory and scrutinising roles over general legislation, Parliament has acquired more substantial powers over financial legislation, now one of its more powerful weapons. Through its budgetary powers, Parliament can impose sanctions on the other Community institutions.

Parliament and the Community budget

Most international organisations are financed by annual contributions from member states. This was originally the case with the European Economic Community and Euratom (the ECSC had its own income, raised by a levy on producers). The Community founders always intended to establish its financial independence, once the necessary resources were available, from levies on the common customs tariff and from the agricultural market, as a step towards freedom from control by the member states. One of the elements of the 1965 Community crisis was the Commission's proposal that revenue from the Common Agricultural Policy should go directly to the Community, providing it with its 'own resources' and that the European Parliament should be granted increased powers of control over the Community budget. This would have been the 'power of the purse' which has so often been the key to parliamentary control of the executive.

French opposition prevailed, but in 1969, in a changed climate of opinion, Community Heads of State and Government agreed at the Hague Conference to the principle of direct financing and new financial arrangements were negotiated in 1970. From 1 January 1979, the EEC budget, that is, the administrative expenses of the Community institutions and the funding of its policies (excluding the European Investment Bank and the European Development Fund), have been financed entirely from 'own resources'. The budget provides the funds for those policies where direct financing has been agreed, for example for the Common Agricultural Policy (nearly all national expenditure on farm support has been taken over by the Community), for the Regional Policy, for cooperation with developing countries and for research. Some Community policies do not involve budgetary expenditure, although they have far-reaching economic implications. There is no Community spending on certain sectors, such as defence or housing, which take up large proportions of national budgets.

In 1979, the total Community budget was equal to just under 3 per cent of the combined national budgets of the member states (about £9,000 million), 43 per cent of the budget coming from a share of VAT in the member states; 40 per cent from the Common External

Tariff and the remainder from levies on foodstuffs imported from non-member states, and also from taxes on the salaries of Community officials. Budgetary contributions are paid in national currencies; budget accounts are kept in a common denominator, the European Unit of Account (EUA) – based on a 'weighted' basket of European currencies worked out on up-to-date exchange rates. In agriculture special ad hoc 'green' rates have been designed to meet particular monetary situations.

Community budgetary procedure is complex. The Commission puts forward policy guidelines for each forthcoming year in March. By June, each of the Community institutions must submit an estimate of its expenditure for the next year to the Commission, which then prepares a preliminary draft budget. This is forwarded to the Council of Ministers in September. Voting on the budget by the Council is by qualified majority. By October, the draft budget must be forwarded to Parliament.

Since 1975, Parliament has been able to reject the whole budget *en bloc* and to call upon the Commission to submit a revised one. It also has the power to amend upwards that part of the budget which deals with 'non-obligatory' expenditure. Expenditure on aspects of Community policies which were set out in detail in the founding Treaties, including the Common Agricultural Policy, come under the heading of 'obligatory' expenditure. At present this constitutes over 75 per cent of the Community's total expenditure. Over this, the Parliament has no direct control. But in respect of the remaining items of expenditure, including spending from the Regional and Social Funds, on energy, industrial policy and information and on the Cheysson Fund which provides emergency aid to countries hit by inflation, Parliament can amend the budget and increase it up to a certain figure, based on various economic criteria calculated annually by the Commission. Budgetary amendments need a two-thirds majority in Parliament.

New procedures for budgetary conciliation were devised in 1975, through which disagreements between Parliament and the Council of Ministers can be resolved. A Committee made up of members of the Council of Ministers and of the European Parliament has a three-month period within which to reach agreement. The conciliation procedure has worked well and is beginning to be applied outside the budgetary field, as a way of introducing a useful dialogue between the two political institutions in the Community. It was through such powers of joint decision-making, that the Vedel Committee saw a chance of progress towards greater democratic control.

A new Community institution, the Court of Auditors, set up in 1977, and appointed after consultation with Parliament, controls and checks that expenditure from Community funds is used efficiently and for the purposes voted. It works closely with Parliament's Public Accounts Committee.

The European Parliament has no say in how Community revenue is raised, historically one of the most important parliamentary powers. But through its existing budgetary powers it can freeze Community spending, and force the Commission to work within the limits of the previous year's expenditure. Its rejection in December 1979 of the entire Community Budget for 1980 was both a political challenge to the authority of the Council of Ministers and a protest at the unbalanced nature of Community spending. The European Parliament was both claiming a greater say in how Community revenue is spent, and also asserting that the level of agricultural expenditure was a threat to the Community's future.

The Community budget is an estimate of expenditure and of the income needed to cover it. There is as yet no budgeting for surpluses and deficits. Except for the CAP the budget only shows part of Community spending, since member states spend large sums separately. Since the setting up of the Regional Fund, the enlargement of the Social Fund and of Development Aid programmes, the Community has moved into areas where spending is intended to influence national production, to control investment, to redistribute income and to reduce differences in the economic and social policies of the member states. The European Budget could be an element in economic convergence and redistributive strategy. At present it does the opposite, due to the CAP which through its effect on price levels, hits poorer Community economies by tending to increase inflation rates. The Parliament, the Commission and most member state governments, would welcome a better balance of Community spending, through the expansion of the Regional and Social Funds and the development of new policies in these areas.

The right to dismiss the Commission

Parliament's powers include the right, so far unused, to take the other Community institutions, the Council or the Commission, to the European Court of Justice for alleged infringements of the Treaties.

It also has the power to dismiss the Commission *en bloc*, by means of a vote of censure passed by a two-thirds majority. This right to dismiss the executive was granted to the Assembly of the European Coal and Steel Community, within which the High Authority was a powerful body, whilst its Council of Ministers was weak. It therefore made sense to give the Assembly the right to sack the High Authority. In the Economic Community, the real centre of decision-making is not the Commission, but the Council of Ministers, over which Parliament has no control. Nor is the right to dismiss the entire Commission one which the Parliament is likely to use (though it has once threatened to do so), since it would cause political disorder. In theory, too, there is nothing to prevent the member states from reinstating the fourteen Commissioners, since they alone appoint them. Parliament does not have, and without amendment to the Treaty cannot formally acquire, the potentially far more useful weapon, the ability to dismiss individual Commissioners for incompetence.

However, Parliament can control the activities of the Commission through less formal methods. Like most modern parliaments its ability to generate public debate, to extract and publish information about the running of the Community, to ask questions, and if necessary, in Barbara Castle's words, to 'raise Hell', is perhaps its most important function.* Since 1973, a Westminster style question-time has been introduced into its proceedings. On the initiative of one of its Committees, political groups, or at least five members, the Parliament can address oral or written questions to the Commission, the Council of Ministers or the Conference of Foreign Ministers. The Assembly also holds debates on the Commission's annual report and other periodic reports, for example on the activities of the Social Fund. Both oral questions and public debate are politically effective, since they force the Commission and the Council to take up a position in public. The Commission in turn has the right to attend and 'be heard' at Parliamentary sittings, an opportunity which is increasingly used by individual Commissioners to make statements on current issues and policies, as by Government ministers at Westminster.

The Commission has adopted the practice of reporting back to Parli-

---

* Barbara Castle, a former Labour Minister, has been leader of the British Labour group in the European Parliament since 1979.

ament on action taken as a result of Parliament's opinions and proposals. The Council too now takes part in Parliamentary sittings. Every six months when the Council Presidency changes, the new President makes a statement to Parliament on future Council policy. The Council, although not obliged to answer Parliamentary questions, in practice usually does so.

Parliament and external and foreign policy
Two Parliamentary Committees are concerned with Trade and Development and also joint Parliamentary Committees have been set up with countries holding association agreements with the Community. Under the Lomé Convention, a Consultative Assembly brings together equal numbers of European MEPs and representatives from the ACP (African, Caribbean and Pacific) countries. Regular joint meetings are held with US Congressmen, Canadian and Latin-American Parliamentarians.

Through the Luns Procedures, Parliament is kept informed by both the Commission and the Council of the progress of negotiations of both association and commercial agreements between the Community and third countries. Parliament would like to acquire the right to ratify all such agreements.

Parliament has no formal powers in the field of foreign policy, which lies outside the Treaties, but it has become involved. The President of the Council of Foreign Ministers holds a quarterly'colloquy' with Parliament's Political Affairs Committee and part of Parliamentary question-time is set aside for questions to the Council of Foreign Ministers. Once a year the Council submits a progress report to Parliament, together with an outline of its proposed future actions; clearly Parliament would like to have more control over the formulation of joint foreign policy initiatives.

The significance of direct elections
The introduction of direct elections may prove to be the most important institutional change since the Community began. For the first time Community citizens became involved directly in Community affairs. But parliaments are not only instruments for ensuring representation 'upwards', they also ensure that governments can mobilise consent. Direct elections strengthened the formal democratic structure of the Community, but only time will tell whether the directly elected mem-

bers will be in a better or worse position than in the past to carry national parliaments and public opinion with them. Part of the job of the new MEPs is to demonstrate to the voters that they are doing useful work in Europe, by publicising important issues and asking questions in Parliament.

The directly elected Parliament meets more frequently and for longer sessions than its predecessor; its research and other facilities have been strengthened and most of its members are new full-time politicians. A number of well-known national political figures have opted for careers at the European level, with eight ex-prime ministers among the members of the 1979 Parliament. There is strong competition for the posts of President of the Parliament and Chairmen of its Committees and there is evidence that the new directly elected Parliament is taken more seriously than the old nominated one.

One of the most difficult tasks of the Parliament will be to work out a common electoral system for the Community of the 1980s. For the first election in 1979, the electoral procedure was left to each member state to work out for itself. Most states settled on a system of proportional representation, relating the number of candidates elected from each party to its share of the total vote. But in England, Scotland and Wales, the 'first-past-the-post' simple-majority electoral system used in national elections was chosen. In Northern Ireland, the single transferable-vote system was used to ensure that the Catholic minority was represented at Strasbourg. The Netherlands, France, Luxembourg, Denmark and West Germany each voted as one constituency, within which the seats were divided between party lists in proportion to the votes cast. Ireland was divided into five constituencies and seats were allocated to each party in proportion to their national vote, reallocated by region according to the regional vote. Belgium's three constituencies were divided according to language between Flemish and French speakers. Only in Britain were members elected to represent specific areas, with local constituency responsibilities.

The first direct election campaign in June 1979 aroused little excitement, yet 110 million people throughout the Community, 61 per cent of the 180 million total electorate, cast their votes. But in Britain by far the lowest number, only 33 per cent of the electorate, went to the polls. In all the member states except the United Kingdom and possibly Denmark, the Community institutions have become an accepted part of the general framework of government; like their national counterparts, they are seen as a necessary evil, useful but far from perfect. British MEPs have the additional job of keeping the electorate convinced that the Community level is worth having at all.

Direct elections brought party politics, virtually for the first time, into the Community system. Members now have to justify their activities in Europe to the party which selected them as candidates and whose supporters elected them to the European Parliament. In Parliamentary democracies the government and the majority of members of Parliament are drawn from the same party or alliance of parties. The party provides a way of holding the government to account for its actions. Until direct elections there was little party rivalry for power within the European Community. Divisions over most issues tended to be national, rather than according to party, and the main Community preoccupations were with the national costs and benefits of Community policies. Parliament itself often played the role of a pro-Europe pressure group. Since direct elections, an electoral campaign has had to be fought and opinions on European issues to be worked out and presented to the public. Parties have had to develop 'European' policies, which should make it easier for the political parties to come together as transnational parties in future, to try to gain power at Community level.

As the Community moves beyond the Treaties into areas in which national political interests are increasingly concerned, right and left-wing differences are likely to become more pronounced, in particular over regional and social policies, where similar political approaches to governmental intervention and to the redistribution of resources are involved. It remains to be seen whether the MEPs will develop strong allegiances, not only to their large constituencies, and to the European party groups within the European Parliament, but also to the transnational union federations and professional bodies whose interests they also represent. It is also possible that political groups at European level may eventually no longer follow national party divisions. They may form on regional, rather than class bases, for example, with Community regions which share particular problems joining forces to protect or to press for their own special interests.[1] Community-level parties may emerge, which, like the American Democratic and Republican Parties, will hardly exist between elections, but will gather at conventions before the European elections are due, to adopt joint European-level political programmes. What does seem clear is that a

Parliament whose members are based full-time in Strasbourg and Luxembourg, and who work through committees which collect information and opinions from sources across the Community on problems with a European dimension, is likely to develop attitudes from which a genuinely 'European' public opinion could grow.

The future of a European Parliament

Formal proposals for increasing Parliament's powers are unlikely to be acceptable to the member states at present, but various suggestions have been made for using existing powers more effectively, for example by more extensive use of the procedure through which Parliament and its Committees can put forward proposals on their 'own initiative', to call upon the Commission or the Council to take action in new areas.

Many suggestions have centred on the effective system of permanent committees, some of which have already begun to hold their monthly meetings in public, when matters of wide interest are under discussion. They have included proposals for subpoena powers, through which the committees could carry out more investigative and pre-legislative work, similar to that of the committees of the United States' Senate, and for research facilities like those of the Library of Congress. A strong Parliament might be able to put enough pressure on individual Commissioners to make resignation customary, should they lose the confidence of Parliament, without formal changes being made to the Treaties. The 1980 Rey Report, one of a series of reports to Parliament on the workings of the Community's institutions, called for Parliament to have a say in the appointment of the Commission and a chance to approve its policy programme.

One suggestion for the long-term future of Parliament proposed a multi-cameral legislature including an economic and social chamber and a regional chamber in which trade unions, enterprises and regional administrations would all be represented.[2] This would accord with the Community's general approach to government in a technological society; that one of its functions should be to promote and to organise concerted action by all the social groups which hold power in society. Many would argue that the European Parliament already gives opportunities for a more professional approach to politics, better suited to the problems of the modern world than, for example, the traditional amateurism of the Westminster Parliament. Prospective candidates already need to demonstrate special expertise in some aspect of Community affairs before they can expect to be considered by their party selection committees.

Changes to the Community's structure

Some adjustments to the Community's institutional framework will be needed before further enlargement. The present institutions, which had difficulty in reconciling the interests of nine member states will find it even more of a problem in a Community of ten or twelve. It has been suggested that as the Parliament becomes more political, the Commission too may need to become a party-political body, with Commissioners aligning themselves with party groups and campaigning on their behalf to get support for the policies they see as essential for Europe.[3] Two 1980 reports on the Community's internal structure, the Report of the Committee of Three (one of whom was Edmund Dell, a former British Trade Minister) and the Spierenburg Report on the Commission, have made similar recommendations. They want to see a stronger, more stream-lined Commission, reduced to only one representative from each country instead of two, with fewer Directorates-General and more departmental coordination and independence from the Council of Ministers, linked more closely with Parliament. The President of the Commission, they believe, should have more control over finance and personnel and more say in the choice of fellow Commissioners.

The Community is an institutional innovation and the system is flexible enough for institutional change to be introduced as and when the member states are ready for it. The Community's founders also believed that the existing integrated functions of the Community, efficiently performed, would attract further support and generate further integration. This process would be helped by the increasing number of national 'actors', lawyers, civil servants, politicians, trade unionists and representatives of professional organisations who would be drawn into the Community's procedures and whose participation in the institutions and advisory bodies of the Community is itself a part of the system. The process is also complex. Any individual or organisation hoping to influence its decision-making has to understand the workings of its institutions and to know where pressure can be applied to them.

PART III   EUROPE OF THE PEOPLE

8 The Community System and the Member States

National participation in Community policy-making

One of the criticisms frequently levelled against central government at national level is that it is too remote to understand and to respond to local needs and priorities. Community membership added a new level to government, even further removed from the grass roots, and one with a strongly bureaucratic and centralised administration from Brussels. Yet at the same time, the Community institutions offer opportunities for participation in policy-making and legislation which in some ways make them more suited to consensus government than do the traditional national processes.

Some of these opportunities are formal and institutionalised. National governments provide the members of the European Council and the Councils of Ministers. The Permanent Representatives and their officials play an important part in transmitting information and documents, preparing negotiating positions, representing their governments in Brussels, expressing the Community point of view to national administrations and in helping to reach Community-level agreements. Within both the Council of Ministers and the Committee of Permanent Representatives there are special advisory committees manned by national civil servants, employers' representatives, trade unionists and others. The Commission too sees the process of *engrenage*, the increasing involvement of national officials in Community decision-making, as a significant way of encouraging a European outlook and of spreading a *communautaire* approach to problems. It consults national representatives at every stage of formulating its policy proposals.

Even in areas where the Commission can make decisions without reference to the Council or the member states, notably in cases within the sphere of Competition policy, it presents its decisions before making them public to an advisory committee of national officials. In this case the British members represent the Office of Fair Trading.

The Economic and Social Committee

All draft Commission proposals which concern economic and social matters must be sent to the Economic and Social Committee of the Community as well as to the European Parliament, for an opinion, prior to their consideration by the Council of Ministers. Employers, trade unionists, farmers, consumers and others are represented on this Committee, which was set up by the Treaty of Rome to replace the consultative committee of producers, consumers and merchants of the Coal and Steel Community. Its 156 members are appointed by the Council of Ministers from lists presented to it by member state governments. They serve in a personal capacity for a four-year term of office. The Committee has powers to initiate its own investigations. It has issued opinions on regional policy, industrial strategy, development aid, consumer protection, the environment and the control of multinational companies. It is widely consulted by the Commission, but is not yet fully used by the Council of Ministers.

Some consultative committees, like the Economic and Social Committee and the Transport Committee, were established by the founding treaties; others have been formed subsequently. Since 1970, for example, a Standing Committee on Employment, composed of the ministers for employment or for social affairs in the member states, representatives of trade unions, employers' organisations and Commission officials has met regularly to discuss employment issues.

Once adopted, many Community policies have to be put into effect by national governments and administrations acting for the Community. Community regulations may involve national procedures; Community directives may need domestic legislation to give them the force of law. The Common Agricultural Policy is administered by national ministries of agriculture, who appoint intervention agencies and collect levies. Customs duties and Value Added Tax are collected by national customs departments. National governments are responsible for settling any disputes which may arise out of the application of the Treaties. The whole system depends upon the collaboration of national administrators.

A new level of government

National practices had to be adapted to allow for Community procedures. Policy-making processes and civil service traditions differ from
country to country, as do national views of the aims and functions of
Community membership. These differences are reflected in the
machinery set up to integrate European policy into government structures.

In France, with its strongly centralised administration and high-
powered civil service, a central committee, the *Secrétariat Général du
Comité Interministériel* (SGCI), answerable directly to the Prime
Minister, was appointed to deal with EEC affairs. It examines and
distributes all documents from the Community institutions, looks at
the implications of Community decisions on French policies and
instructs the French Permanent Representative in Brussels to give
effect to French policy. Community questions in general were seen in
France as part of foreign policy and were made the responsibility of
the Foreign Ministry and of the diplomatic corps. Italy and the
Benelux countries also gave their Foreign Ministers the main role to
play in Community affairs, but in West Germany, policy towards the
Community was originally seen as primarily a branch of economic
policy, for which responsibility was divided between the Economic
Ministry and the Ministry of Foreign Affairs; however, since 1972, the
German Chancellor's Office has begun to play a large part in European
political affairs.

In Britain, a European Unit was set up within the Cabinet Office,
prior to British entry, with a European Integration department responsible for policy towards Europe and for entry negotiations. After Britain
joined the Community, the Cabinet office assumed a coordinating role
on community policy. Within the Foreign Office, two European
Community departments, responsible for Internal and External Community affairs were established and a Political Cooperation Unit was
added later. The Foreign Office is formally responsible for staffing the
Permanent Representation in Brussels, whose officials come from the
Treasury, Department of Trade and Ministry of Agriculture, as well as
from the Foreign Office itself.

In most of the member states, Community affairs, except for politically sensitive policies are settled outside the cabinet, but agricultural
pricing, discussion of economic and monetary union and the

Community's financial resources are usually considered important enough to merit consideration at cabinet level. Britain's tradition of cabinet secrecy and joint responsibility can cause difficulties for individual ministers who need flexibility in Community negotiations.

In all Community countries, membership changed the balance of ministerial importance. Foreign ministers, ministers of finance and of agriculture, trade and industry and customs and excise departments all acquired new responsibilities. Agricultural ministers in particular gained a stronger influence in cabinet meetings.

All government ministers and administrators had to familiarise themselves with European procedures and legislation and with the problems and policies of their fellow members, as well as with each other's languages and traditions. As soon as entry negotiations were opened, the Civil Service College in Britain began running courses in European affairs and Community languages. After signing the Treaty of Accession the then Prime Minister, Edward Heath, called for the 'Europeanisation of Whitehall', but the delays caused by the long-drawn-out membership negotiations and re-negotiations slowed down the process of formulating British policies towards Europe. Certain major adjustments in approach were needed. Relations with other member states became part of domestic politics and government; diplomatic skills were now needed by other departments as well as by the Foreign Office staff and a great deal of the Community's business required a legal outlook.

By the end of the 1970s, well over half the ministers serving in national governments in the member states had already had some experience in European-level organisations.

Community membership and the national parliaments

In each of the member states the national government is answerable to a legislature, which, through a motion of censure, can bring about either the downfall of the government or a change of policies. Under the constitution of the Fifth Republic in France, both Prime Minister and cabinet are responsible to Parliament. In West Germany the Basic Law and Constitution declare the Chancellor to be personally responsible for policy, although there have been recent movements towards collective cabinet discussion and decision-making. In Britain, the Cabinet takes full responsibilities and resigns *en bloc* if censured by a motion of no-confidence carried in the House of Commons.

National parliaments accepted that a transfer of competences took place on joining the Community. Some of the representative functions of parliaments are now performed by the European Parliament. The national parliaments have a part to play in the Community process, for example in ratifying amendments to the Community Treaties. The 1965 Merger Treaty, the 1972 Treaties of Accession, and all association and trade agreements with third countries were so ratified. European affairs are debated frequently, for example in debates on foreign affairs, the budget and economic trends, but the broad effect of Community membership has been to decrease parliamentary and to increase bureaucratic control. In all the member states parliamentary powers in certain areas of legislation are now circumscribed by the existence of the Treaty rules and Community regulations, notably on agricultural matters, trade, some aspects of company law, taxation and regional aid. While questions of Community competence may be debated in Parliament at Westminster, for example, they no longer go through the usual legislative process of second and third readings and Committee stage in the House of Commons.

Governments are required by the European Communities Act to implement directives by statutory instruments. Nevertheless Parliament needs to see that this power is not abused. National parliaments find it difficult to keep themselves fully informed on Community affairs, or to control Community legislation. Most try to exercise scrutiny over European affairs and the activities of Community institutions through parliamentary committees. The Belgian Chamber of Representatives and the Italian Senate have foreign affairs committees which watch over the activities of EEC institutions and their implications. The French have an informal *Groupe d' action pour l' Europe*. In the German system the upper house of the legislature, the Bundesrat, representing the Länder, or regional, governments, has its own office in Brussels.

The Dutch, West German and Belgian Parliaments use their permanent specialised parliamentary committees to build up knowledge about European affairs. The Standing Committees which intervene between the first and second readings of a bill at Westminster have no such specialised competence. In May 1974, two Select Committees were set up by the two Houses of Parliament to survey and analyse the effects of EEC legislation. Documents received from Brussels are sent to these scrutiny committees with a note from the Ministry concerned, indicating their likely impact on United Kingdom law and their potential policy implications. In the House of Lords they go to one of six specialised sub-committees which hear the opinions of ministers, civil servants and others and then report back in some detail to the Select Committee on the European Communities. The Commons scrutiny committee, the sixteen-member Select Committee on European Secondary Legislation, works through all the papers from Brussels and picks out the most important for Parliamentary debate, on a motion to 'take note' of the new measures. But debates on EEC legislation are often held late at night and may be poorly attended. The House of Commons system for monitoring Community legislation has been compared unfavourably with that of the Danish Parliament, whose Market Relations Committee sees all Commission proposals before enactment and all items on the agenda of Council of Ministers' meetings. Danish ministers decide upon their negotiating positions only after consulting this Committee. Its members are influential enough to use sanctions against ministers who exceed their mandate, though obviously this inhibits Danish ministers' freedom to negotiate in the course of European Council meetings.

Direct elections are likely to widen the gap between national parties and parliaments and the members of the European Parliament, most of whom, for the first time, no longer hold a dual mandate. Good relations are necessary if the European Parliament is to become, as it should be, a transnational link, influencing both the national parliaments and the Community institutions. But there could be conflicts if, for example, the European Parliament tried to increase its own powers at the expense of the national Parliaments.

Various suggestions have been put forward for helping European MPs keep their links with national politics during their five years in Europe, for example, that MEPs should keep 'observer' status in national parliaments, or have access to Committees within the home parliament without the right to vote, or that national MPs be invited to work in the Committees of the European parliament. A Select Committee of the Westminster Parliament recommended the formation of a joint 'Grand Committee' of British MEPs, together with members of the two EEC Committees in the Houses of Commons and Lords. It was even suggested at one time that all British members of the European Parliament might be made members of the House of Lords! The European Parliament itself intends to extend its own offices in the national capitals, to help European members keep in touch with national centres of government.

Special interest representation at Community level
From 1953 onwards, groups whose interests were likely to be most affected by the existence of the new European institutions began to set up organisations at Community level. Under the ECSC, the steel producers' organisation (CEPCEO) and the Iron and Steel Workers Federation (FEDERAL) were founded to represent management and workers in those industries. After 1958, most of the main sectors of economic activity followed suit. The agricultural industry is the most integrated and organised interest at Community level. The Committee of Professional Agricultural Organisations of the EEC (COPA), has its own assembly, presidium, secretariat and specialised committees. It keeps closely in touch with the Agricultural Directorate-General of the Commission and lobbies it on measures it wants to see introduced. Commission proposals are studied and debated by it or by its national member organisations. Its representatives sit on the Community's Economic and Social Committee.

Trade and industry have many interests to protect or to promote in Brussels. There are now between 400 and 500 Europe-wide trade associations with headquarters in Brussels. They include UNICE, the European Employers Organisation and a parallel body, the Centre Européan d'Entreprises (CEEP), which represents employers in the public sector throughout the Community. The Confederation of British Industry set up an office in Brussels in January 1971 and is now a full member of UNICE. Chambers of Commerce, the liberal professions, wholesalers and retailers associations, are all represented in Brussels, most with full-time secretariats, all with formal and informal contacts with Commission officials.

Industrial lobbies need to be able to work out a common view and to present a united front to the Commission to negotiate successfully. COMITEXTIL, for example, with between 10–11,000 Community textile firms under its wing, played a considerable part in the negotiations leading to the renewal of the Community's Multi-Fibre Arrangements in 1977. Renegotiation of trading arrangements with the outside world and GATT negotiations often lead to much organised lobbying. Many large individual companies and corporations, for example British Steel Corporation, ICI, and the National Coal Board, have Brussels representation, others have law firms to advise them and to put their briefs to the Commission.

It is not unusual for Commission proposals to originate from within industry. There are now almost forty approved Euro-standards, designed to remove the technical barriers which impede the sale of cars across national frontiers within the Community. Before they were drawn up, the Commission went to the motor industry's associations for consultation about what measures were needed.

Trade unions and the Community

Since the early 1970s, when the Community began to concentrate more on employment and working conditions and on social policy, it has tried to encourage both workers and managements to participate in its policy-making. Where Community proposals affect the interests of workers, with possibilities of job losses, for example, the Commission must consult trade union opinion.

The Trade Unions form the Community's largest organised movement, with 30 million members, but there are many differences between national union movements.[1] In the United Kingdom, the Trade Union Conference forms a consultative 'umbrella' organisation over the movement, while the Labour Party has traditionally acted as its political wing. In most other European countries, the unions individually are more politically active. In Ireland, Denmark and West Germany, they are grouped into one Confederation. In other countries there are separate union groupings according to their political ideologies; Communist, Socialist and Social Democrat and Christian Democrat and Christian. The latter, originally founded to safeguard the spiritual as well as the working conditions of their members, tend to concentrate on wages and working conditions and to oppose radical social change. Social and Social Democratic Unions form the largest group and most of these are linked to Social Democratic Parties. The Communists are more influential in many mainland European trade union movements than in the British: the two largest union confederations in France and in Italy, the CGT and the CGIL, for instance, are both Communist controlled.

In Britain, wage levels are traditionally the main concern of unions; in other Community countries conditions of work are given higher priority than in Britain. In France for example, unions campaign extensively for earlier retirement and higher minimum wages; in

Denmark for co-ownership for workers. In Britain and Ireland, wage bargaining most often takes place between shop stewards and managers at factory level; but in the Netherlands and in Denmark, all wage negotiations are centralised and take place between confederations, employers and sometimes governments.

In post-war Western Europe, the Unions generally were strongly in favour of integration, seeing it first as a way of increasing prosperity and the living standards of their members and later as a means of pooling resources to fight unemployment and to curb the power of multinational companies, the growth of which had presented union negotiators with new problems. Most multinationals are integrated operations, looking for profits for the whole enterprise and ready to move their operations from one country to another to avoid high taxation or strong union pressures. They can step up or decrease the production of individual factories according to the state of industrial relations, or spread their production between factories in the different countries in which they operate. Unions face new obstacles, which they too have begun to realise can only be tackled through cooperation across national frontiers.

It is therefore not surprising that transnational links at Community level were formed in the early days of the Community. The European Confederation of Free Trade Unions (ECFTU) represents the Socialist and Social Democratic Unions; the European Organisation of the World Confederation of Labour (EO–WCL) represents Christian and Christian Democratic Unions. The two major Communist groups, the CGT and the CGIL also have a joint office in Brussels.

From the beginning, the unions, like the employers, were given a part to play in the Community structure, first on a consultative committee attached to the High Authority of the Coal and Steel Community, and later on the Economic and Social Committee of the Economic Community, where they were allocated one-third of the seats. Trade Union groups are also represented on many advisory committees; for vocational training, for the free movement of workers, for health and safety in industry and in the management of the Social Fund. The Permanent Committee for Employment, representing employers, unions and the Commission and member state government representatives was set up in 1970. Joint committees at sector level meet under Commission chairmanship to consider matters of mutual interest. Since 1974, a 'Social Partners Bureau' has been attached to the office of the President of the Commission, to establish regular consultation on matters which include regional development, commercial policy and overseas aid. A European Trade Union Institute, set up under Community auspices, instructs trade unionists in European affairs.

The British Trades Union Congress (TUC) although originally on balance pro-European mistrusted the Community's emphasis on free competition and the market economy and in the early 1970s came out firmly in opposition to British membership. Once inside the Community, they continued to blame Community membership for inflation, high food prices, low productivity and investment, and called for the renegotiation of entry terms. They refused to take up the British allocation of trade union seats on the Economic and Social Committee. The TUC did however collaborate in the formation of a European Trade Union Confederation (ETUC) in 1973, to which Christian and Social Democratic Unions were both eligible, and Vic Feather, General Secretary of the British TUC until September 1973, was elected as its President.

After the referendum in 1975, although disappointed by what they saw as the Community's failure to develop as an effective instrument for tackling inflation and unemployment, the TUC began to play its part in the Community and, in 1977, when the issue of Britain's continued membership was once again raised by the left-wing of the Labour Party, they recommended staying in Europe and working from within the Community to achieve change. Since 1979 both the TUC and the Labour Party have again become increasingly hostile towards the Community. Their reasons include the shortcomings of the CAP, the damage which they believe Community membership could do to British oil interests in the 1980s and the inability of the British government fully to control its own economic policy.

The European union confederations have begun to work out common policies on matters which include full employment, vocational training, harmonised working conditions, hours and holidays. They would like to see Community-level collective bargaining, and contacts between union representatives in the various branches of multinational companies. There is strong support in some member states for worker representation at board level (*Mitbestimmung*) and for the Community directives which attempt to harmonise company law in the member states. Proposals for a European Company and the Commission's fifth directive in 1975 proposing two-tier boards of directors, with workers serving on a supervisory board, received considerable union support, except, notably, in Britain. In 1979, the ETUC Congress, meeting in Munich, declared their intention of working to bring about a general Community-wide reduction of the working week, using, if necessary, coordinated strike action to put pressure on government and employers.

Political parties and the Community

From its beginnings, the Community was supported by the Christian Democratic Parties in West Germany and in Italy and by the Catholic *Mouvement Républicain Populaire* (MRP) in France. Their leaders in the early 1950s, Konrad Adenauer, Alcide de Gasperi and Robert Schuman, were all strong supporters of the movement for European unity. Their parties were associated in the post-war years with progressive social and economic reform. The moderate right-wing parties, the Radicals in France, the Free Democratic Party in West Germany, the Liberals and Monarchists in Italy, all supported the Community. The Gaullists were opposed to the Community at first and their opposition in 1954 contributed to France's rejection of the European Defence Community, but in 1958 de Gaulle accepted the fact of French membership, though the party has since remained in favour of an independent foreign policy for France and of limiting the powers of the supranational institutions of the Community.

During the 1960s, the moderate left, the Social Democrats in the Benelux countries and in West Germany, France and Italy, and the Italian Socialist Party, began increasingly to favour the idea of economic integration. The mainland European Socialist parties, like the British Labour Party, had their origins in the Industrial Revolution and in their opposition to capitalism. But unlike the Labour Party, most have had some commitment to Marxism. In West Germany, for example, the Social Democratic Party's adoption of a programme of moderate social reform and support for private enterprise at Bad Godesberg in 1959, marked a break with a previous long Marxist tradition. The Socialist parties of the six original member states, while never having held power alone, had stood for public ownership of basic industries, and policies of social security and social reform in the coalitions of which they had formed part.

Communists throughout Europe were at first opposed to the Community because of what they regarded as its strongly capitalistic bias.

But in Italy, the success of the European Coal and Steel Community led to a gradual acceptance of working within the Economic Community, even by the Italian Communists. By 1969, Communists from both France and Italy were represented in the European Assembly. In 1972, when the French Communist Party, led by Georges Marchais, formed an alliance with the Socialists and Left Radicals and adopted a common programme, they gave their support to the Economic Community, provided that it could be made to answer more closely to 'the needs of the people'. They opposed the extension of supranational institutions, through which national independence would be lost. By 1976, both the French and Italian Communist Parties had adopted attitudes which became known as 'Eurocommunism', turning away from Soviet socialism and towards Western democratic traditions, in the belief that all industrial capitalistic countries were facing common problems. They looked for a 'fruitful dialogue' with the European left, and continued to take part in the institutions of the Community, in order to protect the interests of industrial workers, migrant workers and small farmers, from within the Community. Communist parties in Western Europe have had to survive the general disillusionment with Stalinism and have experienced the development of mixed capitalistic societies in ways which were not foreseen by Marx or Lenin. Strong national differences remain between the parties. The Italian party's leadership, for example is 'intellectual', while the French is working class and that of Spain more democratically inspired.

Leo Tindemans wrote in his 1976 report that 'only European political parties can bridge the gap between the hopes of public opinion and the powerlessness of governments to turn these expectations into proposals for concrete policies.'[2] Until the introduction of direct elections, national political parties as well as individual voters dealt only indirectly with the European Community, through their governments or national MPs delegated to the European Assembly. Cross-frontier alliances between parties and common approaches to problems developed slowly, until the Community began to be more concerned, in the early 1970s, with policies for employment, income distribution, education and local government. By the mid-1970s European party federations began to emerge.

The Socialist International had set up a liaison bureau for its member parties within the Community as early as 1957 and in 1974 this was renamed the Socialist Confederation. With their wide ideological spread it became increasingly difficult to find common ground, particularly after enlargement, since the Socialist Parties in the three new member states were all to some extent hostile towards Community membership, and there was strong nationally based disagreement over the CAP. However, in 1978 a common 'Political Declaration' was adopted which committed the group to work towards the common goals of European Socialism of 'freedom, justice and solidarity'. The Socialists are pledged to represent the interests of the working man and the consumer. They want to see the protection of the basic rights to health, safety and economic interest by way of a coherent programme and increased budgetary expenditure. But within the Parliament both the German Social Democrats and the French Socialists continue to form fairly close-knit national groups. The British and Italians often have similar aims within the Community and work closely together, as do the British and Dutch. Some Socialists, including the British, Danish and Dutch anti-marketeers went to Strasbourg in order to protect national sovereignty against erosion by any EEC body, and their anti-market attitudes have not so far moderated. The Greek Socialist Party too is anti-Common Market, and is likely to add to the strength of the 'anti' group in the 1980s.

The parties within the Community's Christian and Liberal party groupings are all committed to a more integrated Europe, but they occupy widely different positions with the political spectrum. In Germany, for example, the Liberal Free Democrats are the centre party between the Socialists and the Christian Democrats, whereas in the Netherlands, the Christian Democrats form the centre party. Such differences make close alliances difficult. The formation of the European People's Party (EPP) in July 1976, brought the Community's Christian Democratic Parties together, as well as the Christian Democratic group within the European Parliament. The European Liberals and Democrats (ELD) formed a party in the same year, with Gaston Thorn from Luxembourg as President. A wider European Democratic Union, which the British Conservative Party helped to found, links the centre-right parties from outside the Community as well as within it. Its member parties come from Denmark, Finland, France, West Germany, Greece, Iceland, Britain, Malta, Norway and Austria in an anti-socialist alliance based on support for the market economy and freedom for the individual. The European People's Party advocates greater powers to the Community institutions and eventual political union. European Liberals stress the importance of protecting individual freedom, equal opportunities for all, worker participation in management and the control of undertakings and better use of the regional and social funds, but national differences emerge over the CAP, with German, British and Dutch Liberals putting more emphasis on consumer's needs and the French on the interests of farmers. Fishing and energy issues also divide the member parties. The Communists describe their objective as a 'Europe of the working man' with workers and trade unionists given leading roles in policy-making.

All the party groups represented in the present European Parliament produced manifestoes for direct elections in 1979, but wide differences in national outlooks remained. Only the European People's Party allows direct individual membership and in general shared institutions have been slow to form. National parties are worried that they may lose the control exercised by national party conferences, once European congresses take over. The European Socialists' Congress decisions are binding only if a unanimous decision is reached within the bureau. The Liberals can adopt a European electoral programme if they have a two-thirds majority from their European congress.

In Britain, political parties remain preoccupied by arguments for and against Community membership and over the national advantages or disadvantages to be obtained from the Common Market. Right- and left-wing political views on the Community have not emerged clearly. There is general agreement over the need to reform the Common Agricultural Policy (as there was over the need to reduce the size of Britain's contribution to the Community budget, achieved in 1980), though there are differences over the methods to be used. More pronounced differences may eventually emerge over regional and social policies, with the issues of intervention and redistribution which they involve.*

However the real political dividing line in the Community as a whole remains that between the supporters of a more supranational Community and those who are in favour of an association of sovereign nation states. Although both the European Parliamentary groupings and the European party federations can provide the opportunities for closer integration, it is possible that active transnational groups will

* In 1981 the National Executive of the Labour Party committed itself to leaving the European Community if Labour were returned to power at the next general election.

form more readily outside traditional political parties,[3] from among citizen participation groups, such as consumers, or local government or regional organisations which are looking for a direct link with Brussels to press for urgent objectives. Representatives of regional and ecological or 'Green' parties have already stood for election to the European Parliament.

Local government authorities have felt the impact of Community membership in many areas, such as transport and communications, regional policy, development investment and public health, mainly through Community measures designed to harmonise national law and practice. They too have set up organisations at European level, to monitor and exert influence on proposals for new Community legislation. The two main European organisations of national local authorities, the International Union of Local Authorities and the Council of European Municipalities have a joint office in Brussels. But wide differences between local government systems in the member states have meant that pressure by local authorities on Community institutions still tends to come directly from the national level, either through national local authority associations or by way of central government departments.

Non-governmental organisations and Community lobbying
Since the economic crisis of the mid-1970s national governments have been less willing to spend money on the Community Social Action Programme, set up in 1974, for the improvement of living and working conditions, or on social issues generally. The Commission encouraged the foundation of European-wide independent bodies like the European Environmental Bureau (EEB), the European Bureau of Consumers Organisations (BEUC), the Committee of Family Organisations of the European Community (COFACE), and invited them to produce proposals for action. The International Council of Social Welfare, for example, played an important part in helping to launch the Community's 'Action Against Poverty' programme.

The United Kingdom Government was already well used to working with consultative committees in the public service industries, the National Consumers Council and major voluntary agencies and pressure groups on social issues. In some other European countries the influence of independent organisations is not so strong. Neither France nor Italy attaches the same importance to them as Britain, but in West

Germany, the Netherlands and Ireland they have a similar role to their British counterparts. Once they have joined forces at European level and acquired a sufficient knowledge of the structure and the methods of the Community's institutions and of the formal and informal contacts that are possible with Community officials, they can exert considerable influence on Community affairs. National representative bodies, working through their European-level organisations in direct contact with the Commission, using the Economic and Social Committee and the European Parliament to spread information and to publicise issues, can use lobbying as a means of compensating for the greater remoteness and increased centralisation of decision-making in certain areas, which is said to have resulted from Community membership. Pressure can be applied at so many points, as Community proposals go from Commission to Council of Ministers, by way of the European Parliament and the Economic and Social Committee, that the process has been described as playing 'three dimensional chess'.[4] If the Community were to collapse completely, a network of European organisations would remain, which have become used to working together and have established common approaches to similar problems. The Community system provides an additional level of popular participation in decision-making. In the 1980s the main centres for popular representation remain the national ones, but awareness of the Brussels level of government is growing. The European links have been established and can be extended whenever people are ready to use them.

9 Europe of the Regions

A European view of regional problems

A movement for regional self-government has been part of the general questioning and more critical approach to government and political power in Western Europe since the Second World War. Most European governments have been asked for special help from their regions with particular economic problems and these requests have often been coupled with strong demands for administrative decentralisation and regional autonomy.

The addition of the Community dimension has increased some of the problems of local politicians and administrators, who were unused to dealing with such a remote bureaucracy. But supporters of the European Community believe that while national governments are often forced to adopt policies which are effective nationally, but are not in the interests of particular regions, the Community is in a better position to take an overall view of regional needs. One of the most stimulating effects of the creation of the European Community has been that certain deep-rooted problems, common to most of the countries of Western Europe, can now be seen from a different perspective.

The characteristics of regional problems

The restructuring of European society, begun by industrialisation, gave certain regions huge advantages, as labour and capital were attracted towards the hub of Western Europe, the 'golden triangle', roughly bounded by Birmingham, Dortmund and Paris. Once the Economic Community was established, the central growth area continued to be the industrial area around the Ruhr. The areas furthest away were increasingly disadvantaged, as Europe's wealth and population moved towards the centre.

Seen from a European viewpoint, problem regions have certain characteristics in common. They may be depressed agricultural areas with little industry and high unemployment, like Brittany and mid-Wales and the highlands and islands of Scotland; industrial regions with declining industries and out-dated plant, like the Borinage region of Wallonia on the Eastern Belgian coalfield, or the once-flourishing shipbuilding areas of Clydeside and Belfast; remote peripheral areas like Western Ireland, South-West France and the Mezzogiorno, the southern region of Italy, or border areas like the East-West German frontier zone, where former cross-frontier trade patterns had been restricted. In all of them wages are below national averages and unemployment is higher. There is a high level of emigration and a low level, or rate of growth, of income, and serious deficiencies in 'infrastructure', that is in the provision of transport facilities, water and electricity supplies and other services, upon which economic growth is founded. By contrast, congested urban areas, of which the Randstad, the huge conurbation of Amsterdam, the Hague and Rotterdam in the Netherlands, is an example, have common problems too, though of a very different nature.

In every West European country, successive governments since the Second World War have tried to solve the problems of regional economic disparities: sometimes by the appointment of a special government minister responsible for regional development, or by local government reorganisation and measures to give a certain amount of regional autonomy, or by associating local government authorities with special regional planning bodies.

In Britain, regions needing special help were designated Development Areas and industry was given incentives to set up in these areas. In Italy, a state fund for the South, the *Cassa per il Mezzogiorno* was founded to provide funds for building roads, canals and railways which were needed to encourage industry and to improve agricultural marketing, and state industrial enterprises in steel, oil and petrochemicals invested in the South. In France, financial and fiscal incentive schemes were offered and regional councils appointed to advise on development planning. Cities like Marseille, Toulouse, Bordeaux, Lille and Lyon were named *métropoles d'équilibre* and incentives were provided to attract economic and cultural facilities to them and away from Paris.

Yet despite the economic growth of Western Europe during the 1960s, the problem remained. Emigration in search of jobs took away many of the younger, more active people and made it difficult to improve agriculture or to build up savings for investment in new equipment and better stock. Multinational companies, instead of establishing themselves in such regions often preferred to set up their factories in South America or in the Far East, where labour was cheap.

Community regional policy

The Community Treaties provided for compensation to be given to regions adversely affected by the establishment of the Common Market itself, through the Coal and Steel Fund, which gives grants for industrial conversion and retraining and the European Social Fund. The European Investment Bank has allocated three-quarters of its available grants to investment in poorer areas. But a more comprehensive programme to help the regions would have been against the free market principles widely accepted in the Community in the 1950s and 1960s, that labour and capital should be free to move to areas where optimum output and benefit could be achieved.

By the mid-1960s, the Community had begun to recognise that 'the working of the market mechanism [does] not . . . assure the reduction of differences in regional prosperity'.[1] Regional differences were often greater on a European level than on national ones. Lower Saxony and Bavaria, for example, both received aid from the West German government, but both were rich compared to the whole of southern Italy. An overall Community policy to help the poorest regions was needed.

In the early 1970s Ireland and the United Kingdom joined Italy in demanding a Community regional policy. In Britain in 1973 only the South-East of England reached the Community average in *per capita* income. Other areas of the United Kingdom were below it, sometimes by as much as 20 per cent. The whole of the Irish Republic counted as a development area under the EEC's original plan for regional aid. A Regional Development Fund was set up in 1973 as part of the arrangements for Community enlargement and between 1973–75 a Community Regional policy began to take shape.

The Regional Fund

Since 1975 local authorities in recognised national development areas have been able to submit schemes to their national governments which then select them for consideration for possible financial help from Brussels. The European Regional Development Fund can contribute up to 50 per cent of national expenditure on a given scheme if it is for the relief of agricultural poverty, for industrial change or for the provision of infrastructure. It must be in addition to matching resources provided by the member state government, though this has sometimes proved hard to enforce.

Between 1975–77 the Regional Fund added 15 per cent to the total amount spent by member states on regional aid, with some £540 m. being spent on over 4,700 projects. In the United Kingdom some very large schemes were supported, including the Kielder Reservoir in Northumberland and the aqueduct scheme for bringing water to industry in Tyneside, Wearside and Teesside. A number of smaller projects in Wales were among those to receive assistance, including hotel extensions, roads and sewers for new industrial sites.

In the four years of operation to the end of 1978, the Regional Fund paid out grants totalling over £1,000 m. of which about one-third were for industrial and service sectors, and the rest for infrastructure projects. Nearly three-quarters of the Fund was allocated to the Community's poorest countries, Ireland, Italy and the United Kingdom. For the three years 1978–80, the overall Community budgetary commitment to the Regional Fund was £1,234 m. Although the budget for the Regional Fund is increasing annually, it is not large enough to enable it to transform Europe's regional problems. While agricultural support at national level has been almost entirely taken over by the Community, regional aid merely supplements the aid given by national governments.

Since the recession of 1974, new regional problems have emerged. Structural weaknesses in the economically stronger regions and huge increases in unemployment have led to lower national investment levels in the regions. Paradoxically, with the decline of steel, textile and engineering industries and the return of migrants to rural areas, the economic slump of the 1970s for a time reduced the gap between the richer and poorer regions. But none of them has grown more prosperous and national governments now have even less to spend on the regions.

Some of the Community's own policies have had ill effects on certain regions. Textile agreements with countries in the developing world have increased unemployment in the Yorkshire and Lancashire textile industries. Agreements with Mediterranean countries have not helped the poor agricultural areas of southern Italy. Further Community enlargement is bound to accentuate many regional problems.

The Commission in Brussels would like to see parts of the Regional Fund set aside for use in emergency situations and to offset the effects of certain other Community policies, such as fishery conservation. It would like all the Community's financial instruments, the Regional and Social Funds, the Agricultural Guidance Fund, the European Coal and Steel Community Fund and the European Investment Bank to be more closely coordinated, with Community funds available directly to regional or local authorities, rather than by way of national administrations. Most member states would still find this an unacceptable encroachment on their national prerogatives.

Intervention, redistribution and fair shares
The Commission in a report published in 1977[2] put forward the view that regional disparities at the European level could be eliminated if the Community budget was increased from the 1977 rate of 0.7 per cent of Community GDP to 2.5 per cent, by a transfer of public spending from national to Community level, rather than by actual spending increases. The money could then be used for urban renewal, regional employment, investment subsidies, vocational training etc. The transfer of resources should be an essential part of Community solidarity. Within states, automatic fiscal means exist to redistribute income between regions through personal taxation, public expenditure programmes and social security transfers to poorer regions. In federal countries revenue sharing and grants to provincial governments help to reduce differences between regional incomes. Resource transfer would be an essential part of a full economic union, which remains a Community objective. But to some member states, the transfer of resources from richer to poorer Community economies is still regarded as an intolerable burden and interference. There is strong support in some member states, including the United Kingdom, for a broad balance, or *juste retour*, between what a country puts into the Community budget and what it gets out by way of Community spending. It highlights the differences which exist between those who favour cooperation and the supporters of further European integration.

Moves towards political devolution
Opponents of European integration remain convinced that for the foreseeable future the nation state will remain the unit to which the individual can best relate. Yet in many Western European countries since

the war a struggle for devolution from national governments, or for regional self-government, has taken place, which has occasionally erupted into violent support for more autonomy or even complete independence. In Belgium, where popular identity with the concept of a Belgian nation has never been strong, regional political differences for control of education and local government between the French-speaking Walloons and their Flemish neighbours, have at times almost torn the country apart. Eventually in 1979, the decision was taken to adopt a federal constitution, giving Flanders, Wallonia and French-speaking Brussels each a considerable measure of autonomy within the Belgian state. In Spain, fierce Catalan and Basque nationalism which in the Basque country was supported by a violent separatist guerilla movement, forced the central government to hold a referendum, which again demonstrated overwhelming support for regional autonomy and led in March 1980 to the election of a Basque regional government.

Both Britain and France, the two most centralised countries of Western Europe, with long histories of national unity, have experienced regional political problems. The Northern Ireland problem is unique with its seemingly irreconcilable differences between Catholic and Protestant leading to tragic violence. But even in Scotland and Wales, strong feelings for their distinct and separate cultural and historical identities inspired determined attempts to achieve political devolution, though these received a set-back when referendums held in 1979 resulted in the defeat of proposals for devolved assemblies for Edinburgh and Cardiff. In France, movements for autonomy persist in Brittany, Corsica and German-speaking Alsace, sometimes erupting into violent actions, and many feel that far-reaching powers for the regions may be necessary to prevent campaigns for outright separatism.

In Britain there were some fears that the movements towards Welsh and Scottish devolution could, even by themselves, let alone by exacerbating the Northern Ireland dilemma, lead to the break-up of the United Kingdom. Spain faces similar problems. Yet in West Germany, devolved government seems to have reduced friction between the centre and the regions, and to have helped to stabilise the political system. West Germany's regional (Länder) governments raise half their own financial requirements and have an influential voice in determining the Federal Government's overall economic priorities as well as educational and cultural policy. The Länder-elected representatives to the Bundesrat, the upper house of the West German Parliament, can curb the activities of the federally elected lower house, the Bundestag.

Even where there is little expectation of political union strong feelings of identity with the *petite patrie* have emerged in every Western country since the war, with a revival of interest in minority languages, music and art. The Celtic cultural movements in Cornwall and in the Isle of Man and that of the Occitans of Southern France are typical examples. Many supporters of European federalism see international regionalism, like that of the European Community, and the revival of small nationalities as complementary. They believe that the opportunities offered for local and regional issues to be expressed directly within the Community's institutions, rather than becoming garbled on their progress through national government departments and representative assemblies, outweigh the disadvantages of adding yet another layer to government. Welsh, Bretons, Basques and Catalans are among the groups which have joined the Bureau of Unrepresented Nations founded in Brussels in 1977. In 1978 the Free European Alliance was formed, which included the Flemish Volksunie, the Friesland Party, Plaid Cymru and representatives from Alsace-Lorraine, Aosta, South Tyrol, Corsica and of German-speaking areas of Belgium. They signed a charter for a 'Europe of Peoples', supporting a regionalised and federal Europe. A small number of regional representatives were elected to the European Parliament in 1979. They included a member for Greenland and one from the South Tyrol Peoples Party as well as Winnifred Ewing for the Scottish Nationalist Party and the Rev. Ian Paisley for the Ulster Democratic Union.

Breaking down national frontiers
To some regional federalists the region or province has always seemed a natural basis for a United Europe. Denis de Rougemont, the Swiss writer and federalist described the nation state as the enemy of both local regionalism and European federation, imposing artificial frontiers, which cut across the natural boundaries of language and culture for reasons of economic and administrative convenience.[3]

Since the signing of the Treaty of Rome, daily workers, or *frontaliers*, have been free to move across frontiers within the Community, to work in the nearest industrial centre. Inter-regional associations have been formed for specific projects, such as pollution control, or improvements to the Rhine and Moselle international waterways, and the European Commission supports the principle of joint regional development in transfrontier areas.

To the regional federalist, the regional city or conurbation is a natural unit, reflecting the pattern and concentration of modern growth in population, industry, transport networks and intellectual resources. From a European point of view, for example, the Lille–Roubaix–Tourcoing region is not a frontier zone between France and Belgium, but a transnational metropolitan region, with frontiers extending into Belgium and France, and even possibly into South-East England – particularly if the Channel tunnel is ever built. As administrative units such regional conurbations could be well suited to the political, technical and democratic needs of the late twentieth century. Some theorists would welcome the eventual emergence of a European regional commune within which certain powers to cover a limited range of activities would be transferred to regional authorities with their own executives and elective assemblies. In this way, they feel, more appropriate new centres for political activities and popular participation would be provided than those of the existing nation states, within the framework of the wider European community.

10 European Social Policy

A European approach to social policy

Political systems normally make their presence felt by their citizens by offering services to and making demands upon them throughout their lives. National and local government officials, postmen, policemen, education officers and tax officials provide the citizen with daily reminders of the existence and functions of government. Passports, driving licences, coins, stamps and banknotes have a dual role to play, serving a useful purpose, but also acting as symbols representing governmental authority.[1] So far, the European Community has few such contacts or symbols, although it intends to build up a similar presence and to establish feelings of Community loyalty by introducing a common Community passport, a European driving licence and a common European currency. It is a process which is long overdue. Many of the Community's critics would share the scepticism of Enoch Powell, who was opposed to the introduction of a directly elected European Parliament 'unless and until the inhabitants of different parts of Europe are so penetrated with a sense of their ultimate common interest that they will accept burdens and disadvantages for the benefit of the whole or of other parts'.[2] Leo Tindemans in his report on a possible European Union placed great emphasis upon the need for 'solidarity' among the people of the union. For him and for most supporters of European integration, this could be achieved through action at European level to encourage a fairer organisation of society and to compensate for inequalities of income. A regional policy would help to even out inequalites between Europe's regions. A social policy would protect the rights and improve the living standards of all the Community's people.

A Social Fund was set up by the Treaty of Rome. It was originally intended to retrain and resettle workers who had been affected by economic change. For creating the Common Market was itself bound to cause some problems; jobs would disappear through rationalisation programmes; certain areas would decline in prosperity as modern industries were developed elsewhere; workers would have to be helped to find new jobs or to move to other towns or regions to find work. The European Coal and Steel Community, for example, had already put funds aside for the retraining and re-employment of redundant coal and steel workers. But during the first fifteen years of the EEC's existence it was assumed that the national governments would continue to be responsible for protecting those sections of their own communities which were not benefiting from the increasing general prosperity which the Community itself was helping to produce. There was no broad Community social policy. Interest in social issues remained limited to questions relating to work and employment, the necessary priorities in an economic community.

However, as the Common Market became established during the 1960s and mobility increased, many questions relating to social policy began to arise. Should all Community workers share a common prosperity or were they entitled to higher – or lower – welfare benefits if they moved from one country to another? In the United Kingdom too, public opinion was concerned about foreign use of the National Health Service, and Clydeside and Tyneside shipworkers, considering jobs in Hamburg, for example, needed to know whether they could expect to receive the higher German social security benefits. The Community itself had already begun to take measures to iron out the differences between national standards and working conditions and to assure equality of citizen rights within the Community. But by the late 1960s it was also becoming very clear that in all the Community countries some groups of workers were not sharing in the general rise in living standards. Regional disparities in the patterns of employment were still apparent. Women workers, the handicapped, the young and old and migrant workers were facing employment problems. The Community's own proposals for further integration were likely to increase the need to protect the weaker sections of society. Workers were demanding better health and safety standards and greater job security.

At the 1969 Hague summit conference it was agreed that the Community must be given a more 'human face' with far greater emphasis on social issues. In 1972 a Social Action Programme was agreed upon. A regional policy and measures to protect the consumer and the environment were prepared. All these proposals lay outside the terms of the original Treaties; funds for them would depend upon the political will and the 'generosity' of the member states. The existing Social Fund would need to be reorganised and enlarged.

The proposals which the Commission put forward concentrated on three main areas: the attainment of full and better employment; the improvement of living and working conditions in urban areas; participation in decision-making in industry and in economic and social policy, by management and workers. There were to be special measures to help migrant workers, the handicapped, women workers and other groups regarded as underprivileged.

Within a year of the adoption of this programme, the Community found itself facing the severe economic crisis of 1973–74. Inflation, worsened by the oil crisis and balance-of-payment problems, led to government curbs on public expenditure. The richer countries became less willing to transfer resources to Community funds intended to help countries who, in their eyes, might not be running their economies efficiently. A Regional Fund was set up, but it was much smaller than had been originally planned. The reorganised Social Fund became the main instrument for putting social policies into action.

The reorganised Social Fund

At Dinorwic in Snowdonia, North Wales, a ten-year project by the Central Electricity Generating Board has begun, to build a massive pumped storage system beneath an old quarry. Most of the work force has been recruited from among local people. Many have been trained on courses run by the Construction Industry Traning Board as operators of cranes and earthworking equipment. Young people have been offered mechanical and electrical apprenticeships. A substantial part of the costs of these training schemes and many similar schemes throughout the Community has been provided by the European Social Fund.

The Social Fund is an employment fund. Its purpose as described in Article 123 of the Treaty of Rome, is to improve employment opportunities for workers in the Common Market and to increase geographical and occupational mobility. Since 1973 it has been used to help agricultural workers who are leaving the land, textile and clothing workers obliged to move into other industries or to adapt to new production methods; migrant workers who need vocational and language training; physically or mentally handicapped people; unemployed workers in regions of high unemployment; those under 25, particularly those seeking their first job; workers in industries where updated skills are required; and women over 25 who are unemployed or are returning to work after long absences.

Applications to the Fund have to be approved by national governments. In the United Kingdom the Department of Employment is the point of contact with the administration of the Social Fund. Schemes are selected by a committee which includes representatives of government, unions, employers and the Commission. The costs of an approved scheme may be shared between the Social Fund, the member government and possibly private industry, with the Community contributing in most cases up to 50 per cent of the total. Contributions to the Social Fund are made annually by member state governments according to agreed proportions and must be additional to the amount which each government spends on social policies from the national budget. Since the Fund comes under the non-obligatory part of the Community budget, the European Parliament has considerable control over it and in recent years has recommended increases in the total amounts to be contributed to the Social Fund. In 1978, the Fund's endowment was £381.7 m., more than for the previous fifteen years put together, but in comparative terms, it still only amounted to the sum the Community spent on dairy subsidies under the CAP. Britain's allocation from the Fund was the second largest, £75.1 m., with the largest amount £156.7 m., going to Italy.

Community employment policy
Since 1973 unemployment has become one of the Community's most serious social and economic problems. The Standing Committee on Employment was set up so that representatives of employers and trade unions could meet regularly with the Commission and the Council of Ministers to try to coordinate national policies and to give labour and management a voice in Community employment policy. During 1974 the percentage unemployed among the Community's 100 million workers rose from 2½ to 5 per cent. There were widely divergent unemployment rates between Community countries, from 0.5 per cent of the labour force in Luxembourg to 10 per cent in the Republic of Ireland. By 1981 the total registered unemployed was to rise to nearly eight and a half million people.

Unemployment must in the first instance be the responsibility of national governments, since government expenditure in member states averages 45 per cent of the Community's GNP whereas total Community budgetary spending is less than 0.8 per cent of the Community's GNP. The Community's own employment policy was originally intended to deal with pockets of unemployment in a generally prosperous economy. Like those of the national governments it now had to be adapted to recession and to structural unemployment. The Standing Committee on Employment, the Economic Policy Committee and the Commission, known jointly as the Community's 'tripartite institutions', carry out a programme designed to study the changes brought about by new patterns of employment and investment and to find ways of creating employment. Concerted action to deal with redundancies in the Community's heavy industries, steel and shipbuilding, has been proposed, with schemes for worksharing, restricted overtime and early retirement.

The Commission itself has concentrated on helping the underprivileged groups identified by the Social Action Programme, particularly young people. Unemployment among the under-25s quadrupled within the Community between 1969 and 1979 to well over two million. School-leavers' training schemes, guidance and placement schemes are all eligible for Community aid, as is the education and training of the handicapped. In 1975 a European Vocational Training Centre was set up in Berlin and job creation schemes for young people in health, education, rural and urban development and aid to the elderly have all been supported.

The rights of foreign workers

Among the cases to come before the European Court in 1978 was that of Diamente Palermo, an Italian woman living in France, who claimed that she was entitled to the old-age benefit given under the French social security system to women who have brought up at least five children, although she herself and her children were Italian by nationality. Her right to benefit had been refused by the French courts, but the European Court declared that nationality must not be a bar to receiving state benefits provided the nationality involved is that of a member state.[3] It is one of many cases through which the principle of equality of treatment for migrant workers and their families within the Community is being enforced in the member states.

'Gastarbeiter' or 'guestworkers' from outside the Community countries also poured into the industrial cities of the member states during the 1960s; and in the 1980s over six million immigrant workers live in EEC countries. With their families they amount to about 5 per cent of the Community's population. There are Turks and Yugoslavs in West Germany, North and West Africans in France, Indonesians and Surinamese in the Netherlands. Most no longer regard themselves as guestworkers, but as permanent residents of their new countries, as do the Commonwealth citizens from the Caribbean and the Indian sub-continent who have settled in the United Kingdom.

The original intention of the Social Action Programme was to ensure that no immigrants were exploited and that they had adequate housing and access to the social security, educational and health services of their host countries. Since the 1974 recession serious social problems and local political tensions have arisen. Immigrants are among groups worst hit by inflation and unemployment. All the Community countries are worried by the problem of illegal immigration and by the difficulties faced by countries of origin in re-absorbing workers whose contracts are not renewed by the Community country.

Since 1976, the Social Fund has been able to help member states with funds, for example to train teachers and social workers in the special needs of immigrant families, and to ensure that they obtain their political and legal rights. Through closer coordination of manpower forecasting and of immigration policies with those of trade and overseas aid, it is hoped to sponsor work programmes in the countries from which most of the immigrants come and to strike a better balance between the interests of the Community member states and the countries of origin.

Equal pay for equal work

In 1968 a Belgian air hostess filed a complaint in the Belgian courts against discrimination by Sabena, the Belgian airline. Not only was her salary less than that of a male steward doing the same work, but as a hostess she was obliged to retire at the age of forty, without retirement pay or pension, whereas her male colleagues could work up to the age of fifty-five and were entitled to pensions. When she failed to get satisfaction from the national courts she took her case to the European Court, claiming that Belgian law discriminated against women and was therefore contravening the principle of equal pay for equal work laid down in Article 119 of the Treaty of Rome. The European

Court ruled that the equal pay principle should be applied by the national court.[4] The principle of equal pay is now being incorporated into the legislation of most member states, but progress has been slow. Article 119 was included in the Treaty of Rome to ensure that free competition at work was not distorted by the employment of women at lower rates than men for doing the same job. It was not until the 1970s, when women themselves became more militant, that the Community began to take a more positive attitude to women's rights. In 1975 the first of three directives was issued excluding discrimination in employment, vocational training, promotion and working conditions.

A Community Women's Bureau was set up in 1976 to deal with questions affecting women's employment throughout the Community. Additional help has been made available through the Social Fund to women who were regarded as especially vulnerable to unemployment, particularly the older unskilled or semi-skilled women workers, who can be helped by training schemes to which the Community contributes, such as the British Training Opportunities Scheme (TOPs). One of the aims of the Community's education programme has been to make sure that women have equal opportunities at all levels of education, while the Jean Rey Report on the Community institutions prepared in 1980 called, none too soon, for 'adequate representation' for women on the Commission itself.

Living and working conditions: a Social Union?

At one time the Commission had ambitious plans for furthering integration through harmonising the social systems of the member states.It looked at the possibility of a Community minimum wage and proposals for standard Community unemployment benefits. All Community countries share the common aims of providing access to health and education services irrespective of income, of providing a minimum income for everybody and an insurance system to give security against unemployment, sickness and in old age. However, enormous differences exist, partly due to the cultural traditions of each society, partly to differences in wealth. In Britain, for example, the National Health Service provides medical care for all, whereas in all other Community countries, the health services are organised as part of the social security systems, through compulsory medical insurance schemes, under which either the insurance fund pays hospital and medical expenses direct, as in West Germany, Italy and the Netherlands, or else it reimburses the patient, as in France, Belgium and Luxembourg, usually paying 75–80 per cent of the costs. Pensioners in most EEC countries receive free medical treatment.

In Britain, at least half the cost of the social security system is financed through taxation; in most other countries the employer and employee have to find a much higher proportion of the total cost. Family allowances in Catholic countries are much higher than elsewhere, since large families are still considered to be of benefit to society.

In most existing federations, for example, the United States, it is at federal level that social policies are introduced. But within the European Community, each member state already has a highly developed national social security system. Nearly 25 per cent of GNP in most member states is devoted to social security, whereas the entire Community budget represents only 0.8 per cent of Community GNP. Added to this differences were so great between each country's social benefits and costs of living and there were such strong objections from the wealthier member states at the prospects of financing the poorer, that the Commission finally dropped its equalising proposals. For the foreseeable future, certain differences in social structure, cultural attitudes and values have to be accepted. However, all the member states have experienced a rapid rise in the costs of health and social security services, coupled with demands for more comprehensive social security coverage and further educational provisions. There was therefore a role for the Community to play in identifying common areas of need, establishing common minimum standards and compiling comparative statistics upon which to base further action.

Health and safety standards are clearly common problems for the whole Community. Measures already introduced include the setting of minimum standards for weekly working hours and for annual holidays. A European Foundation for the Improvement of Living and Working Conditions has been set up in Dublin to help in the exchange of information and the setting of standards. A 'Social Budget' was established, to strengthen the Community's statistical resources, with information on matters including employment figures, the labour market, incomes and assets, industrial accidents and rates of crime and of divorce.

The Poverty Programme

In the Surrey town of Croydon, the local Gingerbread Group, a self-help organisation for single parents, has set up a Play Centre for single parent families. For a modest fee, it provides after-school and holiday care for the 5-11-year-old children of single parents in full-time employment. The existence of the play centre has enabled many of the parents to go on to further education and to more responsible jobs. It is part of a joint Family Day Centres Project, coordinated by the Institute of Community Studies, which has been receiving financial help from the Social Fund under the Community's Poverty Programme. The Programme, set up in 1972, aimed 'to test and develop new methods of helping persons beset by or threatened by poverty'. It was an attempt to lift action and research above the national level, to learn from other people's experience and to pool ideas. The results of all the projects will be carefully evaluated by 'Espoir', an independent research unit set up by the Community, but already the Croydon Gingerbread Play Centre has attracted interest from similar organisations in other countries.

The Poverty Programme, though limited in duration and intended only to support pilot schemes, points to the way in which the Community can act as a catalyst and educator, seeking common approaches and pooling ideas for the improvement of social services, provided that the member states are prepared to give its objectives the priority they deserve and the funds to pursue them. The Programme is particularly important because it has involved using voluntary welfare organisations in equal partnership with government bodies. Steering Committees composed of government officials and representatives of voluntary bodies supervise each scheme.

Industrial democracy and participation

Although there has been general agreement between the political parties in Europe over the need for a European-level social policy, the question of the involvement of workers and employers in Community policy-making and, in particular, the relationship of employees to the enterprises which employ them, has led to widespread disagreement. Industrial workers have begun to expect a say in decisions over such matters as long-term investment policy, mergers and take-overs and marketing and production policy, which affect their futures as well as that of the organisation for which they work.

Most European countries have begun to move towards some form of 'co-determination', or board-level representation for workers. In West Germany, Denmark, the Netherlands and Luxembourg, legislation has already been introduced. The Sudreau Commission in France and the Bullock Committee in Britain were both appointed to study and report on worker participation in the management of enterprises. However, British trade unionists have rarely shown the enthusiasm of the businessmen for German-style *Mitbestimmung* regarding it sceptically as 'window-dressing'. They often express views in favour of stronger, specifically Socialist forms of industrial democracy or workers control, but in practice see it as a threat to the power of the unions themselves.

The Community has tried to act as a focus for the exchange of ideas and for the development of a common approach to industrial relations and to the management of industry. Its proposed fifth directive on industrial democracy provides for employee consultation and information about company policies in large companies, with the right of representation at board level. It favours a two-tier board of directors, supervisory and executive, with workers elected from the shop floor to serve on the supervisory board.

Consumer and environmental protection

The creation of the Common Market and the freeing of trade has increased the consumer's choice of goods, but at the same time it has increased the need for consumer information and protection. For a time during the 1960s there was a danger of Community harmonisation for its own sake, with the introduction of standardised products detrimental to consumers' tastes, though the 'Eurobread' and 'Eurobeer' feared by the British press were never a real threat. (The Community's day-to-day business is often humdrum and both press and politicians tend to sensationalise Community issues for their own ends.) Since 1974 consumer vigilance has become an important element in the fight against inflation, and Europe's growing consumer movement has been reinforced since enlargement by the well-organised and influential consumer lobby in Britain.

The Economic and Social Committee has consumer representatives among its nominated members and a Community Consumers Consultative Committee was set up in 1973 to advise the Commission on consumer affairs. It includes representatives of trade unions, cooperative movements and family organisations, as well as consumer associations. The Commission's own Environmental and Consumer Protection Service, set up in 1974, has produced a programme which includes tightening the health and safety standards for foodstuffs and dangerous products, eliminating unfair sales practices, such as misleading advertising and increasing protection for consumers in credit and hire-purchasing arrangements. A special department is to be set up to check for anomalies and distortions in prices across the Community, beginning with the food industry. National consumers' associations are represented in Brussels on the *Bureau Européen des Unions de Consommateurs*, which lobbies the Commission and monitors Community legislation on behalf of the consumer. In Britain the Consumers in the European Community Group was formed in 1978 to represent the views of consumers on all Community activities.

The protection of the environment is another clear area for Community-level action. Over-exploitation of fossil fuels, over-fishing and sea, land and air pollution in any one European country can affect them all. In the Community's 1973 Environmental Protection Programme it was recognised, for example, that industrial pollution does not respect political frontiers. Community-wide measures were drawn up to prevent or reduce pollution, with penalties based on the principle that 'the polluter pays'. Community research programmes have been launched on the effects of tourism on areas of natural beauty, on urban decay, the conservation of ancient monuments, the use of pesticides and the protection of migratory birds. Directives have been produced to protect underground rivers and artesian wells from pollution and to set standards for drinking water. Meanwhile over forty independent organisations throughout the Community have joined forces to form the European Environmental Bureau (EEB) which aims to monitor all prospective Community legislation for possible environmental aspects and a number of 'Green' party or environmentalist candidates stood for election to the European Parliament in 1979, though none was elected.

Part of the Community's job is also to emphasise the collective rather than the national experience of Europeans, while at the same time preserving cultural diversity. Through its education policy, for example, the Community does not try to impose a common education on school-children and students, but rather to promote an appreciation of Europe's shared cultural inheritance. It hopes to persuade educationalists in the member states to give greater priority to language teaching and has produced a syllabus for teaching literature, history and geography from a European, rather than a national viewpoint. It encourages student exchanges and has established the general recognition and acceptance of each national school-leaving qualification for further education throughout the Community. It tries to promote the study and understanding of Europe itself and for this purpose a European University has been set up in Florence, with support from Community funds.

In several cities throughout the Community European Schools have been established where the teaching is conducted in each of the Community languages. At present most of the students are the children of Community officials, but eventually it is to be hoped that such schools will be available for the children of all the Community's migrant workers. On a corner-stone of each school the following words are written:

> The young pupils educated in contact with each other, freed from their earliest years from the prejudices which divide one nation from another, and introduced to the value and beauty of different cultures, will have a growing sense of their common solidarity. Retaining their pride in, and love for, their own countries, they will become Europeans in spirit, ready to complete and consolidate the work that their fathers have undertaken for the advance of a united and prosperous Europe.

They sum up much that is still hoped for from the Community of Europe.

11 External Relations: a Community Foreign Policy?

A recognised international presence

Stable institutions and the cooperation and support of the people who live within it are two essential ingredients for a successful political community. A third is the recognition and acceptance of that community by the outside world.

The city of Brussels, capital of the small state of Belgium, is the headquarters of many international organisations, including two of the institutions of the European Community. By the mid-1970s, Brussels had become one of the focal points of world diplomatic activity and more than a hundred countries had established diplomatic missions in Brussels which were accredited to the Economic Community, regardless of their direct contacts with Belgium itself, or with the other member states. The Community's world-wide recognition was originally due to its success as a trading unit. After its enlargement to ten member states, with a combined population of over 270 million people, much the same as the total population of the United States or of the Soviet Union, it had already become the world's largest trading bloc, accounting for some 22 per cent of the world's trade (excluding intra-Community trade). But the Community also has a growing political authority. Many foreign policy issues are no longer purely national concerns and it has become increasingly difficult for Community states to follow foreign policies which are consistently out of line with those of the other member states. Community supporters hope that through its increasing obligations to consult and to act jointly, a common Community foreign policy will eventually emerge.

External economic relations

The Treaty of Rome excluded foreign policy and defence from its provisions, but it provided for the joint conduct of negotiations in

international organisations and over international treaties, for the
establishment of a common commercial policy towards third countries,
and for the association of overseas colonies and territories in its free
trade and common market provisions.

As a manufacturing and industrial processing area, the Community
needed to export its goods, to open up world markets and to liberalise
trading conditions. The Community's member states were all members
of GATT, the General Agreement on Tariffs and Trade, the United
Nations agency, set up in 1947, to work towards the dismantling of
tariffs, import restrictions, exchange controls and other barriers to
trade. By the late 1960s, when the Community had removed all internal customs duties and established the Common External Tariff
(CET), it was agreed that Community countries should negotiate collectively in GATT and other trade forums. The Kennedy Round of
tariff negotiations which took place in 1966–67 was the first occasion
on which the Commission was given powers by the Council of Ministers to negotiate on behalf of the Community. In 1967 the Community
also began to represent the member states in international monetary
negotiations, when it supported the Special Drawing Rights scheme,
which, through the auspices of the International Monetary Fund,
introduced a new reserve asset to be used in place of gold as a means
of settling payments between countries.

Nowadays, the Community works as a unit in most international
economic negotiations, having worked out a common approach
beforehand. It has its own delegations in Latin America, Japan and the
United States, as well as in the Organisation for Economic Cooperation and Development in Paris. It is represented at meetings of the
Western European Union and the Council of Europe. It has been
granted observer status in the United Nations General Assembly and
the Commission can speak on the Community's behalf in Committee
sessions of the Assembly, though not in plenary ones. In over three-
quarters of all matters debated by the United Nations, the Community
votes as one. During the 1970s it played an active part in the Special
Session of the General Assembly on Raw Materials, in the Conference
on the Law of the Sea, and the World Food Conference. In the Tokyo
Round of GATT completed in 1979, the European Commission
negotiated on behalf of the Nine when a reduction of about one-third
in world-wide tariffs was agreed to.

Foreign trade and commercial policies

The Community set up a network of trading relations which now cover a large number of countries. Preferential and non-preferential trade agreements were negotiated. In both, the Community granted concessions under the Common External Tariff and the Common Agricultural Policy to a range of products from a third country, which offers some measure of reciprocity in return. Non-preferential trade agreements were signed with various states in the Middle East, Asia and Latin America. Under these agreements, the third country benefited from a general non-discriminatory reduction of the CET on a named range of goods of which it was the principal supplier. Most were for a period of three years and were renewable. Preferential Treaties usually entail the reduction of the CET by 50–70 per cent over four to five years and the beneficiary state offers concessions in return. Preferential agreements were originally offered to Israel and Spain, in 1970, and in 1972–73 to the EFTA countries not wanting full Community membership, when industrial free trade areas were created between the Community and Austria, Finland, Iceland, Norway, Portugal, Sweden and Switzerland. A new trade and cooperation agreement signed with Yugoslavia in 1980, improves existing preferential access to Yugoslav products to Community markets and makes low-interest loans available to Yugoslavia over a five-year period through the European Investment Bank, to finance development projects.

Since 1970, the Community has had a common foreign trade policy. The member states agreed to work for a joint Community approach to measures to protect commerce, such as an anti-dumping code and a joint approach to export credit and interest rates. The adoption of the Common Commercial Policy in 1973 has meant that member states are no longer free to negotiate bilateral trade agreements. When existing agreements expire, they will be replaced by multinational agreements negotiated by the Commission on behalf of the Community. Member states retain the right to deal with other types of agreement, cultural, technical, industrial and financial cooperation, defence, security and drug trafficking.

Association agreements

Article 238 of the Treaty of Rome also allows the Community to 'conclude with a third country, a union of states or an international organisation, agreements creating an association embodying reciprocal rights and obligations, joint actions and appropriate forms of procedure'.

Association, which is less than full Community membership, may be preferred by some countries for political reasons. Austria, which is not allowed by treaty to join a political association with other European countries, and Switzerland, with its tradition of political neutrality, have both signed association agreements with the Community. Association may also be an interim arrangement, leading eventually to full membership. The association agreements signed with Greece and Turkey for example were intended to help those countries bring their industrial and agricultural development up to the level of the Community member states before applying for full membership.

A special kind of association was provided for in the Treaty of Rome to give assistance to the overseas colonies and dependent territories of the member states, in particular to the African territories of France, to protect them from losing the trade preferences they had received on the French home market. A European Development Fund was created to give Community financial help to these associated states for infrastructure projects such as the building of roads, hospitals and schools.

When the African states gained their independence during the late 1950s and early 1960s, they nearly all chose to keep their association agreements with the Community. Through the Yaoundé Conventions of 1963 and 1967, a free trade area was established between the Community and the African Associated States. Technical and financial aid included low-rate loans from the European Investment Bank and grants from the European Development Fund. Joint institutions were created, including a ministerial Council and a joint Parliamentary Assembly. In 1969 Association was extended to the three English-speaking African states of Kenya, Uganda and Tanzania.

Preferential tariffs for developing countries
As part of the re-examination of its role in the international community, which took place in the late 1960s, the EEC began to work out a general policy towards developing countries, offering them tariff concessions and development aid. In 1968, when the United Nations Committee on Aid and Development (UNCTAD) called for a world-wide generalised, non-reciprocal system of preferences by the indus-

trialised towards the developing countries, the Community responded by introducing a tariff-free quota for individual manufactured and semi-manufactured goods and for other processed and semi-processed goods from the Third World. The Community's Generalised System of Preferences (GSP) is non-reciprocal since the developing countries are not obliged to offer the industrialised countries advantages in return. It is non-discriminatory since preferences are granted to all developing countries and it is generalised, since preferences have to be granted by all the member states. The scheme has been gradually extended to allow duty-free entry, subject to an annual ceiling, for all industrial manufactures and semi-manufactures from developing countries, and for partial tariff exemption for certain of their processed agricultural products.

When Britain entered the Community in 1973 she had to make satisfactory arrangements for the Commonwealth countries, particularly those in Asia, which were not considered eligible for Yaoundé-type agreements and which would suffer from the ending of Commonwealth preference. The Generalised Scheme of Preferences (GSP) now applies to most goods which would have benefited from Commonwealth preference and the Community has signed commercial cooperation agreements with India, Bangladesh, Pakistan and Sri Lanka (as well as similar agreements with Argentina, Brazil, Mexico and Uruguay in Latin America) aimed at the promotion and development of mutual trade. Joint committees meet to decide upon the most appropriate methods. In December 1979 the Community signed an agreement with ASEAN, the regional grouping of five South-East Asian states, Indonesia, Malaysia, The Philippines, Thailand and Singapore, to explore the possibilities of Community investment in and commercial cooperation with ASEAN countries and the stabilisation of export revenues. Some of its members had also been adversely affected by the ending of Commonwealth preference.

The Lomé Conventions

The 1973 Accession Treaty extended the provisions made for the Yaoundé states to Commonwealth countries in Africa, giving them a similar status to that of the former French African possessions, and to Caribbean and Pacific states with roughly similar economic structure. Forty-six countries including twenty-two ex-Commonwealth countries originally signed the Convention at Lomé in Togo in February 1975.

They were to be known not as Associates but as ACP (African, Caribbean and Pacific) countries. The Convention, which to date covers sixty states, was once again concerned with trade in general, with duty-free access for goods and for financial, technical and industrial cooperation. Most products originating in ACP countries were to be imported freely into the Community, but the Community gave up any reciprocal claims to preferential treatment. ACP countries could charge import duties on products from the Community, though not discriminate between member states.

The Convention introduced the Stabex scheme, a system for stabilising export earnings, through which ACP states are compensated for any loss if the volume of exports to the Community of their most important products falls below a certain level. The Community also agreed to buy large quantities of cane sugar on which many West Indian Islands are almost wholly dependent, at guaranteed prices, similar to those paid to the Community's own sugar producers. Financial and technical projects eligible for Community help are selected by the ACP countries themselves and are managed jointly by ACP countries and by the Community's institutions. A joint Council of Ministers assisted by a joint Consultative Assembly decides on policy. A Committee on Industrial Cooperation and a Centre for Industrial Development were set up to help with the development and marketing of industrial production in the ACP countries.

The second Lomé Convention, to run from 1980–85 extended the scheme to cover full exemption (subject to quota) from customs duties for all industrial goods, and partial exemption for certain processed agricultural products, such as rubber, husk vegetables and oil cake. Its most important innovation was to extend the Stabex scheme to minerals, including copper and cobalt, phosphates, bauxite and aluminium, manganese, tin and iron ore and to introduce measures to promote mining and energy development schemes in the ACP countries. A new Technical Centre for Agricultural and Rural Cooperation was set up, while industrial development and the production of manufactured goods were to be encouraged by larger financial resources. The principle of protection of investment agreements made by European firms against non-economic risks, such as war and nationalisation, was also established.

During the 1960s the EEC was accused of 'neo-colonialism' by some critics in the developing countries. Its policies were seen as a

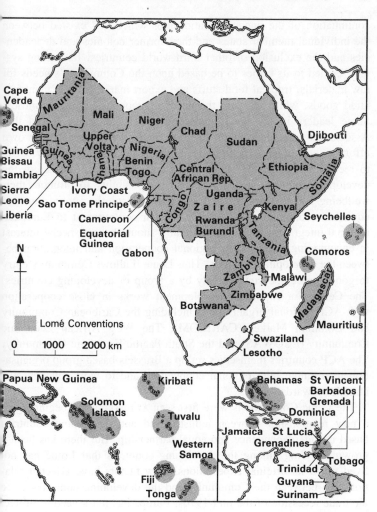

Lomé Conventions

0   1000   2000 km

Cape Verde
Mauritania
Mali
Niger
Chad
Sudan
Djibouti
Senegal
Upper Volta
Nigeria
Guinea Bissau
Guinea
Ghana
Benin
Togo
Gambia
Central African Rep
Ethiopia
Sierra Leone
Ivory Coast
Uganda
Somalia
Liberia
Sao Tome Principe
Zaire
Kenya
Seychelles
Cameroon
Rwanda
Burundi
Equatorial Guinea
Congo
Tanzania
Comoros
Gabon
Zambia
Malawi
Madagascar
Zimbabwe
Mauritius
Botswana
Swaziland
Lesotho

N

Papua New Guinea
Solomon Islands
Kiribati
Tuvalu
Western Samoa
Fiji
Tonga

Bahamas
St Vincent
Barbados
Grenada
Dominica
Jamaica
St Lucia
Grenadines
Trinidad
Tobago
Guyana
Surinam

he ACP countries

continuation of the unequal relationships which had existed between the individual member states and their former colonies and dependencies and the exclusion of other third world countries. Its trading system seemed to its critics to be based upon the Community's needs for raw materials, tropical food-stuffs and export markets for its manufactured goods, while ignoring the needs of poor developing countries. Some leaders in the newly independent African states feared that Association agreements with the EEC might work against their own efforts to encourage African unity. In the 1970s the Community began to recognise that as the largest economic and trading partner of the developing countries it had a special responsibility to promote their wellbeing and to work to 'find and establish jointly a more just and equitable economic order'.[1] With its own commitment to European regional integration it was natural that it should have a special interest in encouraging schemes for regional cooperation and integration between the developing countries. Thus Lomé II allows Community entry to goods processed cumulatively by a group of developing countries. The Centre for Industrial Development works in close cooperation with ACP regional organisations including the Caribbean Community and Common Market (CARICOM), The West African Economic Community (ECOWAS) and the South Pacific Economic Community. The ACP countries themselves set up a Brussels-based group organisation to promote inter-regional cooperation and to work out cohesive attitudes towards the EEC.[2]

The Lomé Conventions were first seen as marking the beginning of a new relationship between industrialised and developing countries based on interdependence and equal partnership. But there has been a growing feeling among the developing countries that Lomé has not lived up to its original expectations. New factors have affected relationships between the Community and the developing countries since the trade recession of the mid-1970s. Europe has felt a need to protect its own ailing industries, in particular shipping, steel and textiles, from the newly-industrialised countries of the developing world: Korea, Hong Kong and Taiwan, for example. The Multifibre arrangements negotiated by the Community in 1977, although generally framed to favour the poorer developing countries, put a temporary limitation on imports of cotton yarn into the EEC at a time when textile products could be stimulating the growth of village industry in many low-income countries. Many developing countries are unhappy about the effects of the Common Agricultural Policy, which in their view makes the developing world worse off by dumping food on world markets and by shutting out Third World food exporters from Community markets.[3] The Community on its side would like to see the developing countries adopt ILO standards regarding hours of work, abolition of child labour in industry and the protection of investment agreements as under Lomé II.

Community development aid

In 1974 Community member states accepted an UNCTAD proposal that the industrialised countries should aim to contribute 0.7 per cent of their gross national product to development aid for the countries of the Third World. Most Community aid is given by way of the member states, though a growing proportion is provided directly through the Community's own instruments, the Budget, the European Investment Bank and the European Development Fund. Much of it is channelled through the regional development banks of the developing countries. The United Nations Emergency Fund, to which Community countries contribute, was set up in 1974 to provide food aid and to organise food production and development schemes in the poorest countries, and the Community itself set up the Cheysson Fund to give aid to countries most badly affected by increases in oil and raw material costs. Food aid may be donated directly to states or through the international organisations, such as the World Food Programme. There are two categories of food aid: emergency aid following national disasters, when the Community supplies goods and transport and pays the distribution costs; and nutritional aid for children, the elderly and refugees who are most likely to be affected by food deficiencies. This food is supplied free of charge to Community ports but the recipient country must cover the costs of transport and distribution. The Community may also supply certain food aids, for example milk powder and butter oil, which can be sold by the recipient countries to finance approved development schemes. Under 'Operation Flood' in India, for example, such supplies were sold and the proceeds used to develop an Indian dairy industry.

After the 1975–76 Conference on International Economic Development, the 'North–South Dialogue', the Community member states agreed jointly to increase their aid efforts and to set up a Common Fund to stabilise commodity prices. But aid programmes have been badly hit by recession and economic stringency. Britain's aid contribution for example, was only 0.39 per cent of GNP in 1980–81. The Commission would like to see Community food aid increased rapidly to meet the growing needs of the developing countries over the coming years with forward planning through a multi-annual programme. But the member states have yet to give the Community the necessary funds or authority to pursue a more long-term or more general development aid policy.

The Community and the United States

In the immediate post-war years the United States encouraged the movement towards European integration to counteract Soviet influence in Europe. The European Community was to become 'a new giant big enough to hold its own in a world of giant powers'.[4] But tensions developed as the Community's strength as a trading unit grew. United States exports to Community countries of commodities covered by the Common Agricultural Policy declined rapidly. Tariff discriminations, preferential trade agreements with third countries and agricultural protectionism became the subjects of major American grievances against the Community.

To Europeans, the activities of private American investment in Europe were now seen as a possible threat to integration and to Europe's cultural and economic identity. American companies operating on a continental scale with massive financial resources, advanced marketing techniques and managerial skills were a threat to Europe's own industries. By 1973, American multinational corporations were producing nearly $300 billion worth of goods abroad each year, more than five times the value of American exports.

The United States no longer exercised the strong political influence over Europe of the post-war years. The Soviet-US acceptance of nuclear parity has lessened the need for American defence dominance in Europe. After the Vietnam War and her internal problems of race riots, student unrest and the Watergate Affair, the United States was no longer the unquestioned leader of the Western World. France in particular began to promote the idea of Western Europe as a potential independent 'Third Force' between the two superpowers. The American connection remained fundamental to European policy, but there was growing sensitivity to direct American domination.

Despite rumbling trade disputes with the United States over cut-price exports of steel to the US and of cheap American chemical products and chemical fibres to Europe, the Community is economically and financially bound to the United States, both for trade and security reasons. Recent American governments have used the need for the American military presence in Europe to obtain economic concessions. Defence remains a crucial issue. France and Ireland now lie outside the NATO command. West Germany is strongly attached to the Atlantic Alliance and is bound by treaty not to develop nuclear armaments. The British have a long history of military cooperation with the United States and want to see a continued American commitment to European defence.

Recent United States administrations' policy towards the European Community itself was summed up by President Carter: 'We should deal with Brussels . . . to the extent to which Europeans themselves make Brussels the focus of their decisions.'[5]

With Japan, as with the United States, the Community's political relations have been good on the whole, but trade has become a cause for great concern. In 1980 Japanese imports into the Community were twice as large as Community imports from the rest of the world. The Community has repeatedly called for improved access for European aircraft, cars and pharmaceuticals into Japanese markets, while Japanese import penetration into European markets threatens to become one of the Community's most acute trade problems in the 1980s.

Relations with the Eastern Bloc and with China

Multinational enterprises now operate across the political barriers between Eastern and Western Europe. East European state enterprises have signed industrial cooperation agreements with West European firms. Renault cars are being built in Rumania with French components, and Fiat cars are made in Poland. Many of Western Europe's political problems, of resource management, labour mobility and citizen participation, are also facing governments in Eastern Europe.

In 1975, the Commission of the European Community was authorised by the member states to conduct joint trade negotiations with state trading enterprises. The Russians are suspicious of the influence of Western European culture and economic attitudes on Eastern Europe. The Soviet Union itself is not a major trading nation, and it does not officially recognise the Economic Community. But recent events have shown that the Russians too accept the existence of the Community, as they see it taking over responsibility for external trade and commercial policy from the member states. By negotiating with the Community over fishing rights within the Community's own 200-mile fishing limits, for example, they gave it practical recognition.

In 1975, the People's Republic of China appointed an Ambassador to the European Community. China has consistently supported the Community which it sees as an element in world stability, powerful and independent enough to resist domination by either the United States or the Soviet Union. The Chinese need steel works, aircraft manufacture and technological help in building up their heavy industries. The Community needs China's minerals, coal, iron ore, uranium and bauxite. A trade and cooperation agreement between China and the Community was signed in 1978.

Community Mediterranean policy

Developments in the Community's agricultural, energy, social and trade policies, and the security interests of Western Europe and of NATO all affect Community relations with the Mediterranean countries. The need to promote political stability in the area through social and economic developments, its strategic importance, and its oil reserves all led to Community proposals in 1972 to develop a more consistent Mediterranean policy, based on three principles: the freeing of trade in industrial goods; removal of restrictions on agricultural trade; cooperation in financial and technical aid, labour relations and environmental protection. Cooperation agreements were signed with the Maghreb states Algeria, Morocco and Tunisia, and the Mashreq countries of Egypt, Jordan and Syria, and with Israel, Malta, Lebanon and Spain.

The imminent enlargement of the Community towards the south is likely to create major difficulties in its relations with the Mediterranean countries, and the Community will have to rethink its Mediterranean policies in the light of that enlargement.

Defence and security

The Community has no military forces and has played no part in the military or strategic aspects of foreign policy. Plans for a common defence policy are made more difficult by the existence of NATO, the separate defence organisation in Western Europe. Eight of the ten member states are full members of NATO. Ireland is not a member, while France has withdrawn from the decision-making structure and has refused to join the Eurogroup within NATO. The member states have competitive armaments and aeronautics industries but proposals for common arms procurement have been made as a way of reducing costs and for operational efficiency. A European Programme Group, which is technically separate from NATO and does include France, deals with the planning of joint production and procurement of military equipment. Inflation and economic crisis have led to reluctance to spend money on defence in the 1970s, but Russian aggression in Afghanistan will undoubtedly strengthen the resolve of many within the member states to establish a Community defence policy in the 1980s.

Conclusions

It was the lack of unity shown by the Community in 1973 during the oil supply crisis which led to the setting up of the Community's procedures for political cooperation based on joint consultation and emergency action at high level. Although political cooperation is increasing and is viewed by many, not least in Britain, as the most promising area of European cooperation, these procedures have not yet become a common foreign policy directed towards agreed objectives. Each member state has a somewhat different geographical and historical outlook on world affairs. Although the Community has become a force in the world, showing considerable solidarity between the member states and gaining benefits for all of them in the process, it still acts as an intergovernmental group in its external political relations, and there is no unified political control. The Community can exert pressure and it can influence world events in ways which have become increasingly difficult for medium-sized powers to do on their own. But such commitments to joint consultation and action do not constitute a common foreign policy.[6] Nor can it become a truly world-level negotiator, until it has developed a fuller range of common policies, in particular over energy supplies and monetary and industrial affairs.

12 Further enlargement of the Community

The entry of Greece and further enlargement to the South

During the 1970s three major European states, Greece, Portugal and Spain freed themselves from dictatorships and established constitutional and representative governments. All three were applicants for membership of the European Community. Backing these new regimes became one of the most important factors in Community political, strategic and economic policies, for once within the Community it becomes more difficult for non-democratic governments to take over again; Greece, Spain and Portugal would need to share in and to contribute to the Community's resources. By acknowledging the inevitability of further enlargement, in order to avoid the political risks of excluding their southern neighbours, the Community demonstrated its acceptance of its own political nature and its concern for the social and political stability of Europe's Mediterranean flank. On 1 January 1981 Greece became the first of the applicant countries to join the Community, as its tenth member state.

The Treaty of Rome clearly states that 'any European state may apply to become a member of the Community'. It does not lay down any conditions of membership. But all the existing member states have certain characteristics in common. They are all mixed economies with multi-party political systems and a free press, with roughly similar aspirations and outlook, able to arrive eventually at some common policies. In addition, in 1978 the Community Heads of State and Government agreed on a 'Declaration of Democracy', which all new members of the Community must endorse as part of their Treaties of Accession. If any cease to be democratic, the Community will have legal grounds for expelling them.

The countries of southern Europe already regard the Economic Community as their natural focus and the opening up of European markets as essential for their further economic growth. Migrant workers to Community countries contribute large sums to their economies. A considerable proportion of each country's external trade is already with the Community. Greece, Spain and Portugal all benefited from the general post-Second World War economic boom in Europe and had similar experiences of movement away from the land, increasing prosperity and an easing of previously rigid social structures. But all were still considerably poorer than the existing member states. Portugal's per capita income is only about one-third of the Community average. All have high unemployment and large agricultural populations and serious regional problems which Community membership could worsen. But although the benefits of joining the Community in the economic situation of the 1980s may not be as great as was previously hoped for, governments in all three countries have accepted the necessity for Community membership not only for the anticipated future industrial and agricultural advantage but above all for the political stability it should bring.

Greece had an association agreement with the Community from 1962 onwards, which covered not only trade, but also a series of preparatory steps towards eventual full membership. It was suspended during the military dictatorship of 1967–74, but in 1975 Greece made a formal application for Community membership. Entry negotiations were completed in 1979 and by the time Greece formally entered the Community on 1 January 1981 most Greek exports were already admitted to the Community free of tax. Under the terms of the Accession Treaty all remaining tariff and quantitative restrictions must be removed in annual stages, so that free trade in industrial goods is achieved by 1 January 1986. Full integration into the CAP will be complete after seven years. However, considerable misgivings over Community membership have developed in Greece, particularly within the Socialist Party. There are worries that Greece might become a satellite Community economy with serious agricultural and industrial problems. There are fears that Greek administrative and bureaucratic arrangements may not be able to handle Community membership and the representation needed at Community level. The Greek Socialist Party is pledged to hold a referendum on EEC membership should it come to power.

Spain formally applied for Community membership in 1977 and hopes to enter in 1984. With a population of 36 million, Spain is already an important industrial power, ranking tenth among the world's industrial nations. The prospect of her entry adds to Community concerns of over-capacity in the shipbuilding, steel, oil-refining, textile and footwear industries. It could cause agriculture problems since she is a major producer and exporter of wine, olive oil, fruit and vegetable produce in which the Community already faces periodic surpluses. She has already begun to restructure her industry, for example, her shipbuilding capacity is to be cut by 50 per cent and steel plants' are to be closed. Spain will need to be more closely consulted on issues involving the 500,000 Spanish workers inside the Community and in discussions about the European Monetary System. The Commission has already proposed that there should be a ten-year transitional period before the full integration of Spanish agriculture into the Common Agricultural Policy.

The then Prime Minister of Portugal, Mr Soares, submitted Portugal's application for Community membership in March 1977, hoping for membership in the mid 1980s; both the weakness of her economy and her relative political instability have proved grounds for a slower, more gradual approach. An agreement on Associated membership between Turkey and the Community also allows for a transition towards possible full membership, by the mid-1990s. Turkey is regarded in much the same light as Portugal. It is necessary to help her from the point of view of foreign policy. But her membership would cause great economic problems at a time of recession in the EEC as a whole.

The total population of the Community of Ten is approximately 270 million and the entry of Spain and Portugal would add another 44 million people to the Community. Most of them live in areas which are as poor as the poorest regions of the existing Community. The member states, although giving qualified approval to continued Community enlargement have some misgivings. France, which sees some advantages from becoming a more central power within the Community once the countries of Southern Europe are added to it, is apprehensive about the impact of southern wine, fruit and vegetables on the CAP and on French agriculture in general. West Germany supports further enlargement, but is worried about additional costs, of which she might have to bear a large share. The Dutch and Belgians are anxious about increasing the difficulties of reaching decisions in the enlarged Community, and Britain, Ireland and Italy, the poorest Community countries, are concerned about the possible loss of revenue to them from the limited resources of the Regional and Social Funds and competition from the textile, steel and motor vehicle industries of the Iberian Peninsula.

A further problem concerns the ability of the Community's institutions to support enlargement. A Community speaking nine, instead of the existing seven, Community languages would increase the burdens on the administrative machinery. Council meetings might last even longer and package deals be even more difficult to achieve. The Dutch and Belgians insist that reforms to the institutions should come before further enlargement, in particular, relaxation of the veto in the Council of Ministers, and the substitution of qualified majority voting on such issues as rules for migrant workers and the use of the Social Fund. The new entrants would have problems in dealing with imports from the developing countries which are already allowed in under the Community's existing treaties. Community relationships with the developing world and with other Mediterranean countries will be affected. The strategic position of Greece in the Eastern Mediterranean already raises military and political questions. The quarrels between Greece and Turkey could cause difficulties for the Community. Also at present neither Spain nor Turkey recognises Israel, which has close Treaty links with the Community. But positive advantages of enlargement to the South include the closer trading and cultural links with parts of Africa, South America, the Middle East and the Mediterranean which would follow. Portugal, for example, could bring the Community more closely into contact with her former colonies in Africa and with Brazil, and Spain with the other countries of Latin America. Greece has already contributed her large merchant shipping fleet to that of the Community and her existing commercial and shipping links with Arab countries and the Balkans are a new Community asset which the Greek government described as 'the dowry which we bring with us as a new EEC member'.[1]

Enlargement to the North?

Enlargement of the Community to the North seems unlikely in the foreseeable future. Although both Sweden and Norway are politically and economically eligible for membership, neither is likely to consider it in the near future. In Norway, the referendum rejecting membership in 1973 was decisive. Sweden's traditional neutrality is a major obstacle. Both keep close links with Brussels and are associated with it through trade, while Denmark often acts as a bridge between the Community and other Scandinavian countries. EFTA and OECD also provide opportunities for the discussion of many issues.

The implications of further enlargement

For the next twenty years, the Community is likely to be greatly preoccupied with the changes that will become necessary as a result of further enlargement. Enlargement to the South will extend the Community's frontiers to include the southern limits of Western Europe and will add to its world stature. But once again there will be new members with their own interests and priorities to pursue and it will inevitably become a different, less homogeneous kind of community. Enlargement could slow down integration and the Community's ability to act decisively in world affairs, at least while the new countries are being assimilated, or it could force it into accepting a much more definite common foreign policy and to emerge as a European superpower.

13   Energy Supplies and Industrial Policy

The most worrying and immediate problems throughout Europe in the early 1980s remain the economic ones. Mass-unemployment, inflation and monetary instability, scarcity of energy resources and industrial decline threaten all the European countries alike. The European Community is still first and foremost an economic community, yet it cannot take common action over economic policy as a whole. Inflation and unemployment are in the first instance the responsibility of the member state governments, which have far greater resources available to deal with them, than the Community has from its small budget. But the Community can try to ensure that member state policies all have the same objectives. Extensive consultations take place between Community Economics Ministers. Joint economic policy guidelines are prepared, together with a programme for medium-term economic policy.

Energy policy and 'oil politics'

Community policy has always been to encourage economic growth as a stimulus to employment. But economic growth is dependent upon many factors, one of the most important being plentiful energy resources. Although the Community founders recognised that a secure food supply was an essential foundation for economic and social progress, they failed to acknowledge the equal importance of energy. Until the early 1970s, plentiful energy resources were taken for granted, even though the Nine were already importing 60 per cent of their energy needs and over 80 per cent of their oil from outside the Community.

In 1973, when the Arab-Israeli conflict was followed by massive oil price increases the Community was divided. The member states tried to secure their own separate supplies through bilateral agreements with the oil producers. Some countries introduced temporary rationing, others suffered temporary shortages. There was little joint Community action to share out existing supplies or to guarantee them for the future. The Community Heads of State and Government, meeting in Copenhagen in December 1973, agreed that a comprehensive Community energy policy had become essential in order to reduce the Community's reliance on imported energy, to share out existing energy supplies in the event of future supply crises, to plan a Community programme of energy conservation and rational use and to enable the Community to negotiate jointly with the oil producing countries.

At the North-South Conference on Economic Cooperation between the countries of the Third World, the OPEC oil producers and the industrialised countries, and at meetings of the International Energy Agency, the Commission negotiated on behalf of the member states. It drew up plans for increasing Community coal production and nuclear energy capacity, for developing natural gas production for reducing petrol consumption and for developing new energy resources. But little concerted action was taken since the member states continued to put their own domestic energy problems first. Britain was determined to keep control of her North Sea oil and Italy of her cheap coal imports from Eastern Europe. France gave priority to her nuclear expansion programme, while in Denmark, West Germany and the Netherlands, widespread political opposition to nuclear power developed for environmental reasons. Ireland was anxious to catch up with the rest of the Community in her economic development which would inevitably increase her energy consumption.

There was still no real Community policy on oil and petroleum product supplies, over 90 per cent of which were now being imported from outside the Community, nor towards coal production, the Community's own plentiful but expensive energy resource. Coal producers within the Community still face difficulties because of the import of cheaper coal.

In 1979, the Iranian Revolution once again showed up the Community's vulnerability when oil supplies were again disrupted. This time it became clear that the forecasts of dearer and scarcer oil supplies by the end of the century had been optimistic. World-wide energy shortages had already arrived to stay.

Community energy policy again became a priority. The Heads of State and Government agreed to impose a 5 per cent energy saving on

Community energy consumption. Oil imports were to be reduced to 1978 levels by 1985, and alternative energy resources were to be developed as rapidly as possible. National energy policies were to be coordinated, and assistance given to Community common projects. The Community agreed to finance oil prospecting in developing countries, to train staff and develop technologies for converting coal into hydrocarbons. High oil prices had made research into new energy resources an economic proposition and the Commission began research projects into geothermal and solar energy, coal gasification and liquefaction as well as into energy-saving projects.

But so long as Community member state governments are unwilling, for national political reasons, to give the Community a more decisive role in directing an energy supply policy the real needs of a Community-wide energy policy, of persuading the Community's consumers to use more Community-produced coal, of settling the question of access to North Sea oil, of making decisions about the contribution which nuclear power should make to Europe's energy supplies, and of how to dispose of nuclear waste, will remain unsolved, together with many related problems, such as the need to increase public transport, to switch to the production of smaller cars, even to make reductions in the working week.

The Community's Agricultural Policy was originally developed through intergovernmental bargaining over the needs of French agriculture and the expansion of European industry. If a comprehensive energy policy were to develop in the same way, then Britain with her North Sea oil resources could hold the key. To many Europeans, Britain is acting selfishly by not giving price or supply preferences to her partners in Europe. Common Community oil prices, supported above world prices by levies similar to those introduced as part of the CAP could encourage Community producers to produce more domestic fuel supplies.[1]

A policy for industry

With its past emphasis on the development of the CAP and of the Customs Union, the Community has not acted as decisively as it could do in many other areas which need Community-level action. In the 1980s it will need not only to spend more on securing energy supplies, but also to support industrial employment.

Industrial prosperity and growth has been one of the basic conditions for economic and social progress within the European Community, but Community industry in the early 1980s is facing crisis. The wider market for industrial products offered by the Customs Union had allowed industrial production to increase by 63 per cent between 1963–73. But since then the Community's industrial growth has begun to slow down. Between 1974–79 industrial production increased by only about 11 per cent,[2] while the level of unemployment rose from 2.5 per cent to 6.2 per cent. By mid 1981 nearly eight and a half million Community workers were unemployed and the numbers were still rising.

The price of oil and of the raw materials needed for industry has increased astronomically since 1974. International monetary instability has hindered industrial development. Competition from newly indus trialised countries and the introduction of high-technology industries which need large-scale investment and a wide industrial base have transformed the industrial scene in Europe.

Some aspects of industrial policy have a natural European level since they involve large-scale investment to sustain them. Certain industries involve Europe-wide strategic planning; the development of energy resources and transport, for example. Some need the weight of the Community behind them to negotiate effectively with the produc ers of energy and raw materials. Other industries are facing difficulties caused by over-capacity, and if unemployment is not to be 'exported' from some to other Community countries, over-capacity, for example in the steel, textile and shipbuilding industries, have to be tackled jointly.

Helping declining industries and developing new ones

When the European Coal and Steel Community was founded, the coal and steel industries were two of Europe's most important industries since they supplied the energy and raw materials for most industrial activities. Today both these industries are in difficulties throughout the Community. Europe's steel faces competition from Japanese, South Korean and Spanish industry. Plant requires modernisation and surplus capacity has to be cut back.

The Community had adopted the Davignon Plan, named after Vis count Davignon, the Community Commissioner responsible for indus trial affairs, which is intended to help restructure the steel industry and to create new jobs in areas which have specialised in steel production in the past.

Problems facing the textile, shipbuilding and footwear industries have also been approached on a European-wide basis. The Community negotiated on behalf of the member states to reach a Multifibre Agreement, by which low-wage textile producing countries agreed to voluntary restraint' agreements on exports to Community countries. It is trying to promote new technologies in the aerospace, data processing and electronics industries. Under Euratom it is initiating research into new reactor types, and into the development of safety standards and regulations for the storage of waste. It can help areas suffering from industrial decline, through contributions from the Social and Regional Funds, but these actions are piecemeal and there is not yet an overall Community common policy.

Research and development

New high-technology industries, such as aerospace, data processing and telecommunications require skills for which Europe's workforce and long industrial experience are well suited.

The new industries of automation and robotics, information techniques, nuclear technology, space telecommunications, the development of new energy resources and the study of the environment all require huge investments which can only be carried out economically and efficiently on a Community-wide scale. Japan and the United States are already far ahead of Europe in research and development in these areas. The Community has a research programme which concentrates on life and information sciences': energy resources, measures to improve competitiveness in agriculture and industry, links with developing countries and the development of information technology and the use of leisure. But an overall view of policies and priorities is needed, of the future structure of industry, of developments in science and technology, of regional distributions of manpower and employment and of long-term prospects for energy and raw-material supplies. Moreover if a common European industrial policy is to be achieved an Economic and Monetary Union will eventually prove inescapable.

14 Economic and Monetary Union

The Incomplete Common Market

Over twenty years after the inauguration of the Common Market, frontier posts still exist between the member states and Community citizens have to show their national passports at many inter-Community
frontiers. Although the last of the tariffs on inter-Community trade
were abolished in 1977, goods and people still cannot move freely
Until national laws are fully harmonised, Customs officers will have to
go on collecting VAT and excise duties, seeing that animal and plant
health regulations are carried out, controlling immigration and carrying out many more duties besides. Conditions of trade in the member
states are still far from equal, while considerable differences still exist
between national taxation and monetary policies, company law and
export aid schemes. Differing rates of inflation and varying exchange
rates create uncertainty between member states. A Customs Union
must inevitably lead to attempts to harmonise taxation, budgetary and
exchange rate policies and eventually to complete economic integration.

The implications of economic and monetary union

Economic and monetary union would involve a very large transfer of
power from the member states to Brussels. It would mean a single
Community currency, Community control of national monetary
policies and massive transfers of funds to the Community budget
Since different levels of economic development and resources exist
throughout the Community, it would mean transferring wealth from
one part of the Community to another, with additional protection for
areas with difficulties. Regional, social and industrial policies would
all have to be greatly extended. The political implications are enormous, involving the virtual surrender of the rights of member states to
manage their own economies. The Community institutions would

have to assume responsibility for steering the joint economy, controlling interest rates, employment and taxation levels and the money supply. Supporters of integration would like to move rapidly towards economic and monetary union, which they believe would lead to eventual political union.

The founding Treaties did not commit the Community to an Economic and Monetary Union, although they did call for the coordination of economic policy, and the setting up of a Monetary Committee 'to review the monetary and financial situation of member states'. Little was achieved in working out common monetary policies before 1969 because of inflation and exchange rate instability, although committees were set up to discuss budgetary policy, medium-term economic policy and central bank policy. Major changes in the international monetary system and in the world economy made economic policy integration very difficult. In 1969 France ran into balance-of-payment difficulties and devalued the franc; the Germans revalued the mark in the same year. Currency disturbances led to Community proposals in December 1969 for closer economic and monetary union. Pierre Werner, Prime Minister of Luxembourg, was asked to look at ways of harmonising monetary and fiscal policies in order 'to realise an area within which goods and services, people and capital, will circulate freely and without competitive distortions, and without thereby giving rise to structural or regional disequilibrium'. He proposed a complete Economic and Monetary Union, including a common currency, by 1980, to be achieved in three stages, during which currency differences would be gradually narrowed and eventually locked.

His plan quickly ran into difficulties. Community opinion was divided in its approach to economic policy. Should a common currency precede or follow long-term convergence of economic and budgetary practice? In France there was strong support for monetary union to counter dollar influence in Europe and as a means of achieving reform in the international monetary system. But a common currency and fixed exchange rates would give little freedom to individual governments to choose their levels of unemployment or growth rate. Both Britain and France were concerned at the loss of national control which would be involved in economic policy coordination, while the Germans insisted that coordination should precede any steps towards a monetary union.

A crisis was caused by the decision of the United States to move off the gold standard in 1971, and this was quickly followed by the 1973 oil crisis and the beginning of a long period of world monetary disorder. Community member states drew back from cooperation and tried to control their own economies. It became increasingly difficult to hold national economic policies together and all hopes of a complete Economic and Monetary Union by 1980 had to be abandoned.

However some steps towards closer cooperation were taken. Central banks in the member states were allowed to run up short-term debts in each other's currencies; and in 1975 the Community raised a loan on capital markets to help member states with balance-of-payment deficits caused by high oil prices. The European Monetary Cooperation Fund (FECOM) was set up in 1973 to form the nucleus of a future Community central bank system and a decision-making centre for Community economic policy, somewhat on the lines of the US Federal Reserve system.

The European Snake

In 1972 attempts were made to narrow the margin of exchange rate fluctuations between Community countries. The European Exchange Agreement created a monetary mechanism, christened the 'Snake', through which fluctuations between Community currencies were to be regulated with a maximum permitted fluctuation of 2.5 per cent. Eventually it was hoped to eliminate these fluctuations entirely and it was expected that a *de facto* European currency would emerge from the elimination of market fluctuations and exchange rates.

Member state central banks began to support each other's exchange rates against the dollar. But due to inflation, the instability of the Italian lira and of the pound sterling, the joint Community float was soon in difficulties. In June 1972, Britain and Ireland were forced to leave the Snake, followed by France and Italy, when pressure on their exchange rates became intense, reflecting the increasingly wide range of rates of inflation and the varied pace of economic development in the member states. The countries left within the Snake formed a German mark area in international monetary affairs, working outside the Community's institutions.

The European Monetary System

In 1977 Roy Jenkins, then President of the Commission, became convinced that moves towards monetary union were essential if Europe's central economic problems of high unemployment, low investment and inadequate growth rates were to be solved. He proposed a single European currency, to co-exist with present national currencies, replacing them gradually as it became more acceptable, and a central authority to manage monetary policy.

After some initial scepticism, the proposals were taken up by Helmut Schmidt, the German Chancellor and President Giscard d' Estaing of France, and a new plan to stabilise the currencies of the Nine was put forward and eventually adopted in March 1979. A new zone of monetary stability was to be created, backed this time by the creation in 1981 of a European Monetary Fund, a common fund to contain one-fifth of the member states' reserves of gold and dollars, to provide more money for market intervention. A European Currency Unit (ECU) would act as a reserve asset and as a means of settlement. Each participating currency would have an ECU related central rate to be used to establish a grid of bilateral exchange rates.

Both French and West German opinion accepted that without currency stability there could be little chance of reducing inflation and creating the conditions needed for sustained growth in world output. For West Germany, with her export-centred economy a stable mark was considered essential. In France, it was hoped that a stable franc would give the government the chance to impose wage and price restraints on French industry and trade unions. The Benelux countries and Denmark, still members of the original Snake, saw the proposed European Monetary System (EMS) as an extension of what they were already doing.

In Italy, EMS was regarded as a major step towards economic and monetary union and towards the development of the European institutions. Italy and Ireland were offered and accepted a looser arrangement within the system which allowed wider currency fluctuations against the new central rates. All the Community member states except Britain joined the system.

Britain, although associated with various aspects of the scheme including the partial pooling of resources (she will allocate 20 per cent of her reserves to the central pool) has not become a full participant. British governments fear the surrender of their freedom to manipulate exchange rates; if their currency was pegged to the West German mark British manufacturers might be priced out of the market. Many people in Britain would prefer a closer coordination of economic policies, in particular aid from the strong Community economies like West Germany for weaker economies like those of the Irish Republic and Great Britain.

Monetary union

Full monetary union would involve the setting up of a European Central Bank and a European Treasury. It would mean taking two important instruments of economic management out of national hands and putting them in the hands of the Community. National governments, although free to decide the level and composition of public expenditure and taxation, would have the monetary framework within which these decisions were taken laid down for them at the centre. Member states would no longer be free to devalue their currency against other Community currencies. Above all it would need a politically controlled Community executive and a Parliament with strong enough powers to supervise and direct it.

It is hard to imagine the Community member states agreeing to such a step in the near future, with the political decision-making it would involve at Community level. But the achievement of economic and monetary union remains a major objective of the Community. Without it, the eventual establishment of a European Union will not be possible.

15 The Common Agricultural Policy in the 1980s

Britain and the Common Agricultural Policy

Britain always knew that the Common Agricultural Policy would be expensive. Since the proportion of the population working in agriculture was less than in the rest of the Community (3 per cent in Britain in the early 1970s compared with an average of 16 per cent in the rest of the Community), and as a major agricultural importer Britain would have to pay out large sums to cover the cost of the Community's agricultural system, compared with buying on the world market as previously. Consumers would have to pay farmers the difference between Community and world prices, which the Exchequer had paid previously.

Under the British agricultural system, before she joined the European Community, British farmers received a direct subsidy from the government, known as a deficiency payment, when market prices fell below a guaranteed level, fixed annually by farmers' representatives and the Government at an Annual Price Review. This was intended to add enough to the market price to cover production costs and to give farmers a reasonable income. The system of deficiency payments and grants towards efficiency meant that consumers were paying world prices and supplies did not expand overmuch. It was designed for an agricultural industry which did not attempt to meet all the needs of the market. In the Community, where self-sufficiency was one of the objectives of the agricultural policy, which had already been achieved in many products, such a system would be too expensive. When Britain joined the Community her deficiency payment system was phased out and British policy was brought into line with the Community system. She expected industrial and political gains from Community membership, and it was hoped to bring about changes to the agricultural policy from within the Community.

In fact Community enlargement in 1973 coincided with a period of high world food prices. For a short time a situation of world grain shortages was encountered, coupled with sharp increases in the costs of fertilisers, fuel and machinery. Exports were taxed and imports subsidised and Community consumers benefited from below-world-market food prices, especially in sugar and grain. A controlled market and a policy of encouraging domestic production were shown to be beneficial at a time of world shortages. By 1975, world food prices began to fall again, but while sterling was weak, British consumers obtained some benefit from the Community's newly introduced 'green money' system.

Green currencies and Monetary Compensatory Amounts

The Common Agricultural Policy was formulated during the 1960s on the assumption that national currencies would remain stable, but in 1969, faced with French and German devaluation and a subsequent general floating of exchange rates, the Community was forced to act to protect the structure of the Community agricultural market, based as it was on common price levels throughout the Community, equal market intervention and equal levies. Community agricultural prices were expressed in a notional currency, referred to as an agricultural unit of account (AUA) which had an agreed value in terms of each of the national currencies. Monetary instability made it necessary for the Community to intervene to hold the AUA at its original parity. Currencies held at these artificial parities for agricultural purposes became known as 'green' currencies. 'Green' rates of exchange protect farmers in strong currency countries and consumers in weak currency countries. Regular adjustment of the rates would ensure that prices did not differ greatly between member states. But in practice this has not happened since national Governments have tended to keep their green rates out of line with market rates of exchange for considerable periods of time, thus in effect deciding their own price levels. Border taxes and subsidies (called Monetary Compensatory Amounts, or MCAs) are paid between the member states to maintain these different price levels. MCAs and currency instability have meant that agricultural prices have differed widely between the member states. In 1979 for example British prices were 30 per cent below those of West Germany.

Since 1974, the CAP has been generally badly affected by the Community's economic problems. Member state governments have been forced to grant subsidies to domestic agricultural sectors hit by crises. Import levies on milk products and restrictions on beef imports, export levies on sugar and cereals have eroded free trade in agricultural produce.

Overproduction and high costs

Over the first six years of membership it was estimated by the *Cambridge Economic Review* that British food prices had risen by about 12 per cent in real terms as a direct result of the CAP. Most of the 150 per cent rise in British food prices during that period was attributable to rising world prices generally and to increases in the costs of production, processing and distribution.[1] Nevertheless British food prices, like those of the other member states, are kept up by the high level of support prices which the Community pays its farmers. In 1976, for example, butter was 220 per cent higher than on the world market, wheat 124 per cent and beef 158 per cent. The CAP also encourages overproduction; since it aims at self-sufficiency in many products, some surpluses are inevitable. Community farmers produce all they can, knowing it will be bought off them by Community intervention authorities if the open market fails. One of the main areas of overproduction has been in dairy produce, consumption of which is falling, while Community milk output continues to rise. The cost of subsidising dairy surpluses uses up to one-sixth of the total Community budget. The system of intervention buying works well for grains, cereals and sugar, most of which can be stored indefinitely and moved relatively easily. But livestock products present storage problems. As a result thousands of tonnes of butter have been exported at cut prices to the Russians and others, or stored in refrigerated ships off the French and Irish coasts. Huge quantities of milk powder have been fed to dairy cows. Public anger following press reports of growing butter mountains, wine lakes and cut-price intervention sales led to the introduction of subsidised butter and beef for pensioners and those on social security, but consumer pressure for changes in the system continues to grow.

From the beginning the Common Agricultural Policy was geared to give the average farmer an income equivalent to that of an industrial worker. Farm prices were set high enough to give farmers in poor areas a profit. As a result large and efficient farmers in rich areas have over-produced and over-earned. In West Germany, where there are many small and inefficient farms and part-time farmers, the support needed to bring them up to the industrial levels of prosperity is very high indeed. Nor has the policy solved the problems of the growing income gap between rich and poor farmers throughout the Community. In Southern Italy, France and Western Ireland, rural poverty continues. But in Northern Europe, big farming cooperatives, commodity trading and food processing companies have made massive profits out of agriculture. Export subsidy schemes sometimes give opportunities for fraud, with the same cargo going from port to port collecting subsidies. Butter sold cheaply in Eastern Europe has been reimported into the Community; whilst in Ireland, pigs are rumoured to spend much of their lives trotting back and forth across the border between Northern Ireland and the Republic collecting subsidies as they go!

With further enlargement, the number of Community farmers could increase by half as many again. Greece, Portugal and Spain are all dependent upon agriculture for employment and foreign exchange. Spain produces the equivalent of 25 per cent of the Community's vegetable crop, grown more cheaply than within the Community, since salaries and welfare costs are lower. Extending the Community's market support system to the full range of Mediterranean produce would result in astronomical extra costs.

Reform of the Common Agricultural Policy

Market management and price support policies were never intended to be the whole of the Common Agricultural Policy. It was always expected to include measures to improve farming techniques and marketing systems and the services and facilities of rural areas. Larger, more efficient farming units were to be encouraged with fewer people working on the land. Over its first fifteen years, for example, the number of farmers in the Community was halved and productivity considerably increased. The Guidance Section of the Farm Fund reimbursed member states for part of their expenditure on modernisation. In 1968 the Commission introduced the Mansholt Plan for agricultural reform and in 1972 a Farm Development Scheme and a Pension and Amalgamation Scheme were set up. Grants were given to owner-occupiers who gave up farming, to assist them in finding jobs in other industries. Small farmers were encouraged to amalgamate, and marginal land was re-allocated for forestry or tourism. Lower agricultural prices can be achieved, if farming standards are raised, but it is a slow process and structural reforms are expensive.

Since the late 1970s, the position of agriculture in the Community has changed. While agricultural productivity has continued to rise, consumers spend less of their incomes on food. The average expenditure per household on food 'fell from 40 per cent to 25 per cent between 1966–75. More milk products, beef and sugar are produced than people want to buy. In addition, the fall in the number of agricultural workers has led to depopulation in some rural areas. Special measures have had to be taken to provide more rural jobs and to help special areas, such as hill farming districts, through the Regional Fund.

The farm lobby has become less powerful since the Community was enlarged and the consumer's voice has grown stronger. There is a general feeling throughout the Community that the CAP must be reformed. At the beginning of the 1980s almost three-quarters of the Community's budget was being used for farm support, to buy, store or dispose of food surpluses grown by farmers who made up less than 8 per cent of the Community's work force. The Community presents a protectionist wall against outside producers. While millions of pounds are spent on Community stockpiling, the aid available to its own poorest regions and sections of society, and to the poor in the developing world must necessarily be reduced.

The CAP is still the Community's most important single practical policy. Its objectives – security of supply, stabilised markets, a steady income for farmers – remain valid, but in all the member states there is concern about the increasing costs of agricultural support and the need to reduce surpluses and costs to consumers. Prices need to be reduced to levels which reflect the cost of production by efficient producers. It seems likely therefore that farmers themselves may be asked to bear more of the costs of the agricultural policy despite their electoral importance in several member states. Many no longer need the support which it has given them and some of those who do could be helped through expanded Social or Regional Funds by way of selective benefits.

The decision of the European Parliament in December 1979 to reject the Community Budget for 1980 was partly a protest against the overwhelming proportion of the budget devoted to the CAP, described in an article in *The Times* newspaper as 'the cuckoo which is progressively ejecting the other birds, such as the regional and social policy, from the Brussels nest, through its voracious appetite for funds'.[2] Since Britain is a major food importer, the Agricultural Policy was also largely responsible for Britain's own disproportionately large budgetary contribution (a major Community issue until a more equitable interim arrangement was reached in 1980), through the common customs and tariff duties. With her own small agricultural industry, she' receives little by way of return benefits from the policy.

By 1982, the Community's budgetary expenditure is likely to exceed the revenue available for financing it from the present arrangements. The entry of Greece and the re-negotiated Lomé Conventions have increased the strain on the budget. Some member states will be unwilling to increase their contributions unless a better balance can be achieved within the budget itself and in particular over agricultural spending.

Conclusions

The case for a regional grouping

'Brief as it is, the history of the European Community is the sum of its crises. It might also be described as a process of development *in* crises and through them', wrote Willy Brandt in his memoirs.[1] There will always be controversial issues which cause difficulties between the member states and which slow down progress towards further European integration for months or even years at a time. Nor is Western Europe – the area to which the Community, after the further enlargement to which it is committed, will approximate – likely to be entirely self-sufficient in the foreseeable future. For defence and security reasons, for example, it will need wider alliances. The Community is also unlikely to take over completely from the governments of the nation states of which it is composed. These have recovered their prestige and authority and continue to hold the loyalty of their citizens to an extent which was not anticipated by the post-war federalists.

Developments in modern society, however, are leading to the acceptance of the 'multi-tiered' approach to government, with functions being carried out at the lowest level compatible both with efficiency and with accessibility for those whose needs it serves. A regional grouping like that of Western Europe can form a unit large enough to act as a necessary balance between the rival superpowers. But such a grouping must give each member state benefits which it can no longer achieve on its own. It must perform only those functions of government which cannot be carried out better at lower levels, closer to the individual citizens. Like every other level of government it must allow for diversity of development within the group, for the maintenance of human rights and for individual participation in decision-making.

Roy Jenkins, then President of the European Commission, speaking in Florence in 1977, accepted this need to limit Community action to areas where the European level alone is effective. Among them he included policies which require a natural European level for treatment because they involve strategic interests which cannot be split between the member states, in particular energy and transport policies, nuclear security and pollution control. He named certain industries which can offer particular economies of scale if organised on a Community-wide basis: aerospace and telecommunications, automation and robotics, as well as industries linked to Community trade policy because of excess capacity: steel, textiles and shipbuilding, and financial policies including Economic and Monetary Union which help to fight inflation and which will lead towards fuller integration of the European economy.

The Community system

Since the late 1960s, the Community has had to find ways of moving forward in increasingly difficult circumstances. It has become more pragmatic and adaptable, abandoning for the present the idea of a full federation, in favour of trying to persuade the member state governments of the merit of certain European solutions. It has moved forward slowly, as politics and circumstances have allowed, not by planned stages. With its own institutional framework and its powers and functions shared with the member states, its unique *sui generis* system, it is engaged in moving towards what has been described as 'an open ended system of functional integration'[2], rather than a formal European union.

Its progress has been uneven, since its policies are often piecemeal, lacking in effectiveness because they are incomplete or are restricted by national political sensitivities. It now seems likely that in future, in Shirley Williams' words, 'events will compel togetherness...'. Europe will have to work more closely together to avoid 'bloody battles over a diminishing supply of raw materials, energy and agricultural supplies'.[3]

The Community's functions, like those of all government in the modern world, can be described as to stabilise, to coordinate and to modernise: to provide a 'dynamic continuity in an environment of change'.[4] Community policy makers, like those of their national counterparts, have to adopt a flexible approach to the various institutional mechanisms available to them. In certain policies, where continental-level bargaining is needed, for example in commercial relations with third world countries and in monetary negotiations, direct management by the Community will be needed. But there are also policies which have both a Community and a national element, such as social harmonisation, where the Community can continue to exercise its supervisory and educative role, or where existing instruments such as the Agricultural Management Committees and the Central Banks Committee can be developed to achieve joint action.

A European federation or confederation?

In his memoirs Jean Monnet described the European Community as 'only a stage on the way to the organised world of tomorrow'. Federalists have not given up the idea of world government – a federation of federations. To some, the European Community will never be a world power until it has a Senate representing the member states, a House of Representatives representing the citizens, a Supreme Court and a Constitution on American lines. They are cheered by the existence of a working European bureaucracy and an elected European Parliament, all this within thirty-five years of the Second World War. They point out that it took the United States seventy-five years to become a full federal union. In the multinational and multilingual European Community the time span could be much longer, since the member states were already well established, with centuries of independent development and rivalry behind them before the Community began.

Others see the present Community moving in the direction of confederation and point out that the Swiss and German Federations, as well as that of the United States, were preceded by long periods of confederation. They are aware of the continuing strength of nationalism in Europe and of the concern paid within the Community since 1965 for national interests and priorities, and the growing development of formal machinery for political cooperation rather than the integration of member states. They see the Community evolving into a coalition of nation states pursuing common interests, rather than conforming to a supranational model.

The future of Europe

At the end of his long life, so much of which was devoted to the European cause, Monnet summing up his own view of Europe's future in the world, wrote of the difficulties of foreseeing today the decisions that will be taken in a new context tomorrow.

The essential thing is to hold fast to the few fixed principles that have guided us since the beginning: gradually to create among Europeans the broadest common interest, served by common democratic institutions to which the necessary sovereignty has been delegated. This is the dynamic that has never ceased to operate, removing prejudice, doing away with frontiers, enlarging to continental scale, within a few years, the process that took centuries to form our ancient nations. I have never doubted that one day this process will lead us to the United States of Europe; but I see no point in trying to imagine today what political form it will take. The words about which people argue – federation or confederation – are inadequate and imprecise. What we are preparing through the work of the Community is probably without precedent. The Community itself is founded on institutions and they need strengthening; but the true political authority which the democracies of Europe will one day establish still has to be conceived and built.[5]

A European identity

Clearly a true European political community will not exist until pressure for action at the European level comes from the citizens of Europe. Public opinion needs time to adjust to and to accept a new level of government. In much of mainland Europe, young people in particular already accept their European, alongside their German, Belgian or Dutch identities. But in Britain, suspicion of Europe remains strong. Jack Jones, the British trade union leader, once accused pro-Europeans of looking at the Community through 'wine-splashed spectacles' and the average Briton remains unconvinced of any pressing need to cross the Channel other than for a fortnight's annual holiday in the sun. Many Englishmen are more interested in and knowledgeable about political life in the United States than they are about that of their European partners. To many, the European Community seems to belong exclusively to the bankers, the businessmen and the lawyers and it is only gradually, through the opportunities of working together which the Community processes do provide, that farmers, fishermen, trade unionists, representatives of welfare organisations or consumers groups, as well as members of the European Parliament are beginning to understand and to appreciate the advantage of a joint approach to shared problems.

The individual states which have joined together to form the European Community have a common culture and a great deal of shared experience to draw upon. At the same time they are both politically and economically mature enough to retain their individuality and to resist the dangers of uniformity. The Community offers them new structures through which to tackle certain common economic and social problems, some security through joint action at a time of economic and political uncertainty and a chance for the people of the Community to share more fully in and to add their own contributions to Europe's rich and varied cultural heritage.

The philosopher Ernest Gellner[6] has argued that in the modern world there are only two universally valid claims for legitimacy that states can make. One is that those in authority should be 'co-cultural with the ruled' in the sense of being of the same 'nation' and not alien rulers. The other is that they are successfully raising the living standards of their people, in a qualitative rather than a quantitative sense. Both these conditions must be satisfied if they are to retain the loyalty of their members. Ultimately a European Community can only succeed in creating the former if it is successful in this latter objective.

Notes and References

Chapter 1. From Federalist Idealism to Common Market

1. See Karl W. Deutsch, *The Analysis of International Relations* (Foundations in Modern Political Science series, Prentice Hall, 1968) p. 158 and Leon Lindberg and Stuart Scheingold, *Regional Integration* (Harvard University Press, 1971) p. 6.
2. Altiero Spinelli, 'European Union and the Resistance', in *Government and Opposition*, vol. 2, no. 3 (April–July 1967), reprinted in Ghita Ionescu (ed.), *The New Politics of European Integration* (Macmillan, 1972).
3. Quoted by Arnold J. Zurcher, *The Struggle to Unite Europe 1940–58* (Greenwood Press, 1958) p. 6.
4. See Charles de Gaulle, *Mémoires de Guerre, vol. III, Le Salut*, pp. 57–8, quoted by Richard Mayne, *The Recovery of Europe* (Weidenfeld & Nicolson, 1970) p. 69.
5. Quoted by R.C. Mowat, *Creating the European Community* (Blandford Press, 1973) p. 61.
6. Richard Mayne, *The Community of Europe* (Gollancz, 1962) p. 62.
7. *The Memoirs of Sir Anthony Eden: Full Circle* (Cassell, 1960) p. 32.

Chapter 2. The Economic Community 1958–73

1. *The United Kingdom and the European Community*, Cmd.4715 (HMSO, 1971).
2. The Maillet Report, see Ghita Ionescu, *Centripetal Politics* (Hart-Davis, 1975) pp. 150–4.

Chapter 3. The Community and Political Issues During the 1960s

1. Charles de Gaulle, *Mémoires d'Espoir, Le Renouveau 1958–62* (Wiedenfeld & Nicolson, 1971) pp. 178–9.
2. See Uwe Kitzinger, *The European Common Market and Community*, (Routledge & Kegan Paul, 1977) pp. 184–5.
3. From *An Introduction to International Law* by J.G. Starke, 8th edn (Butterworth, 1977) p. 113.
4. Peter Jenkins in *The Guardian* 7 June, 1975. See also Philip Goodhart, *Fullhearted consent: the story of the referendum campaign* (Davis-Poynter, 1976) p. 181.

Chapter 4. The Enlarged Community of the 1970s

1. Michael Shanks in *The Social Policy of the European Communities*, a special issue of *Common Market Law Review* (Sijthoff, 1977) p. 3.

Chapter 5. A New Legal Order
1. D. Lasok and J.W. Bridge, *Law and Institutions of the European Communities* (Butterworth, 1973) p. 38.
2. For example *Costa* v ENEL, Case 6/64, European Court of Justice. See Roy Pryce, *The Politics of the European Community* (Butterworth, 1973) Ch 3; Roger Broad and R.J. Jarrett, *Community Europe Today*, rev. edn (Wolff, 1972); and for more detail P.S.R.F. Mathijsen, *A Guide to European Community Law* (Sweet & Maxwell, 1972) on the nature of Community Law and the work of the European Court.
3. Reaction by the Republic of France to a 1979 judgment which prohibited French import restrictions on lamb was one such exception.
4. See Andrew Shonfield, *Europe: Journey to an Unknown Destination* (Penguin Books, 1973) pp. 23–7.

Chapter 6. The Roles of the Commission and of the Council
1. See Richard Mayne, 'The Role of Jean Monnet', in *Government and Opposition*, vol. 2, no. 3 (April–July 1967), reprinted in Ghita Ionescu (ed.), *The New Politics of European Integration* (Macmillan, 1972).
2. At the time of writing, proposals are under consideration to reduce the number of Commissioners to one per member state and to reduce the number of Directorates–General (see p. 78).
3. 'Report of the working party chaired by Professor Georges Vedel examining the problem of the enlargement of the powers of the European Parliament', *Bulletin of the European Community*, Suppl. 4/72.
4. Agricultural proposals go to the Special Committee on Agriculture.

Chapter 7. The European Parliament and Democratic Accountability
1. See the paper read to the Law Society of Scotland Conference on European Law, 9 Feb. 1978, by Professor John Mackintosh, MP.
2. See 'The European Social Partners' by Ghita Ionescu in *Federal Solutions to European issues*, edited by Bernard Burrows, Geoffrey Denton and Geoffrey Edwards (Federal Trust, 1978).
3. See David Marquand, 'Towards a Europe of the Parties', *The Political Quarterly*, Oct.–Dec. 1978.

Chapter 8. The Community System and the Member States
1. See James Barber, 'Trade Unions in the Community', in *The European Economic Community: Work and Home*, Units 7–8 of an Open University Post Experience Course (Open University, 1974).
2. In *Europe Bulletin*, published by the European People's Party in June 1976.

3. See A. Hartley 'Transnational Political Forces' *European Community: Vision and Reality*, edited by James Barber and Bruce Reed (Croom Helm and Open University, 1973).
4. By David Buchan, 'How Industry can put more Clout into EEC Lobbying', *Financial Times*, 16 Aug. 1978.

Chapter 9. Europe of the Regions
1. *EEC Medium Term Economic Policy Committee Report*, 1966.
2. *Report of the Study Group on the role of public finance in European integration* (EEC Commission, Brussels 1977).
3. See Denis de Rougemont, *Lettre Ouverte aux Européens* (Paris, 1970).

Chapter 10. European Social Policy
1. The first part of this paragraph is based upon a speech made by Roy Pryce, director of the Community's Information services to the International Political Science Association, in 1976.
2. Rt. Hon. J. Enoch Powell, MP, in a speech given at Market Drayton, 6 June, 1969.
3. Toia, Case 237/78 European Court of Justice.
4. Defrenne, Case 43/75 [1976] European Court of Justice.

Chapter 11. External Relations: a Community Foreign Policy?
1. Council of the European Communities, *Twenty-fifth Review of the Council's Work*, 1977 (Brussels, 1978), p. 105.
2. See 'The European Community and Regional Cooperation in the Third World' by Carol Cosgrove Twitchett in *European Cooperation Today*, Kenneth J. Twitchett (ed.) (Europa, 1980).
3. See *The C.A.P. and the developing countries*, a World Development Movement pamphlet (London, 1978).
4. Walter Hallstein, *United Europe, Challenge and Opportunity* (Oxford University Press, 1962) p. 67.
5. See William Wallace, 'A Common European Foreign Policy: Mirage or Reality?' in *Federal Solutions to European Issues*, edited by Bernard Burrows, Geoffrey Denton and Geoffrey Edwards (Federal Trust, 1978) p. 183.
6. William Wallace, *op. cit.*

Chapter 12. Further Enlargement of the Community
1. See article by John Cooney in *The Irish Times*, 3 January, 1981. p. 6.

Chapter 13. Energy Supplies and Industrial Policy
1. See John Pinder, 'Europe the Next Five years', *New Europe*, Summer 1979.

2. From 'Monthly Industrial Short-term trends', UK Department of Industry, Statistical Department, June 1980.

Chapter 15. The Common Agricultural Policy in the 1980s

1. See *Food Prices in the European Community* published by Consumers in the European Community Group (UK), 29 Queen Anne's Gate, London, May 1979.
2. Michael Shanks, 'Controlling the Cuckoo in the Nest', *The Times*, 29 Dec. 1979.

Conclusions

1. Willy Brandt, *People and Politics: The Years 1960–75*. (Collins, 1978) p. 239.
2. Donald Chapman, *The Road to European Union*, Sussex European Papers (University of Sussex, 1975) p. 34.
3. Shirley Williams in an article in the *New York Herald Tribune*, 7 June 1979.
4. Tom Ellis, 'Why a Federal Britain?' in *Federal Solutions to European Issues*, op. cit., p. 48. On the functions of government see Ghita Ionescu in *The New Politics of European Integration* (Macmillan, 1972).
5. Jean Monnet, *Memoirs* (Collins, 1978) translated by Richard Mayne, p. 523.
6. Ernest Gellner, *Thought and Change* (Wiedenfeld & Nicolson, 1964) p. 33.

Select Bibliography

There is already a large and growing literature on all aspects of the European Communities. Much of it is both detailed and technical. Since this book was intended to provide an introduction to the subject for the student and for the general reader, I have concentrated on texts for the non-specialist. Most provide the necessary bibliographies which will lead the reader on to more detailed studies.

The simplest and clearest recent guide to general sources of information about the European Communities is *The European Economic Community: A Guide to Sources of Information*, compiled by Gay Scott ALA, Information review no. 3, Capital Planning Information (London and Edinburgh, 1979). *Sources of Information on the European Communities* by Doris M. Palmer (Mansell, 1979) is also helpful. *A Guide to the Official Publications of the European Communities* by John Jeffries (Mansell, 1978) covers official publications only.

The most fruitful source of information about the European Communities is the publications office of the Community itself. It publishes many different levels of material in all the Community languages. They include wall charts and simple pamphlets, like the 'Who?, What?, Why?, How?, Where does Britain Fit in?' recently prepared for schools by the Communities' London Information Office, as well as all the Community treaties and official reports, many excellent background series and a wide range of statistics. They are available from the London office of the European Communities at 20 Kensington Palace Gardens, London W8 4QQ, which also has a reference library open to the general public and a knowledgeable and helpful staff. Among the series which the general reader might find particularly useful are the *European Documentation* pamphlets on main Community policies, the monthly *European File*, and *Europe 81*, a new monthly magazine published by the London office. More detailed information is available from the various Annual Reports of the activities of the Communities, for example, the *Report on the Development of the Social Situation in the Community* and that on Competition Policy. The annual *Facts and Figures* provides an up-to-date source of basic statistical information, and in 1980 the second selection of statistics on Community social conditions and trends *Social Indicators 1960–78* was published by the EEC Statistical Office.

Exploring Europe is described as a magazine for the 16–19 age range which aims to provide detailed study of topics of importance to life in contemporary Europe, using source materials and experts to set out the main points of contention on a chosen topic. The first three titles were *The European Parliament*, *Rural Depopulation* and *Nuclear Energy*. The series replaces the excellent background series *European Studies* on which I have drawn extensively

ınd with gratitude. It is published by the Schools Unit, Sussex European
Research Centre, University of Sussex, in association with the Commission of
he European Communities.

Newspaper coverage of Community affairs tends to concentrate on topical
ssues and does not always have sufficient space to supply the full background
o current news stories, though both the *Financial Times* and *The Guardian*
ıre usually informative and the regular European Community section of *The
Economist* is invaluable, *The Economist's* 'School Briefs' sometimes cover
Community topics and their EEC Election Briefs which appeared before the
European Election campaign in April and May 1979 were particularly useful.
The Journal of Common Market Studies (Blackwell) and the *Common Market
Law Review* (Sijthoff and Alphen, Noordhoff, Netherlands) publish current
ıcademic and legal studies on the Communities.

Two standard works which between them cover most aspects of Community
Studies are Roy Pryce, *The Politics of the European Community* (Butterworth,
1974) and Dennis Swann, *The Economics of the Common Market* (Penguin,
1972). At a similar level on the Community in general is the Open University's four-part Post Experience course published in 1974: *History and Institutions: National and International Impact; Economics and Agriculture*; *Work
ınd Home*, and its accompanying volume of readings *European Community:
Vision and Reality*, edited by James Barber and Bruce Reed (Open University,
1974). *The Community Today* (Commission of the European Communities,
English edition 1979) was written by a group of European civil servants to
provide young people in their final years of school with background material
on Europe today. It was originally intended for use in Belgian schools.

The personal memoirs of contemporary European statesmen who helped to
form the European Communities include those of Jean Monnet, *Memoirs* (Col-
ins, 1978) translated by Richard Mayne, Willy Brandt, *People and Politics:
The Years 1960–75* (Collins, 1978), Charles de Gaulle, *Mémoires de Guerre*,
3 vols (Collins, 1955–60) and *Mémoires d'Espoir* (Weidenfeld & Nicolson,
1971), together with Harold Macmillan's volumes of memoirs (Macmillan,
1969–73).

Many standard texts cover the history of post-war Europe and the following
ıre particularly useful for providing a clear account of the events leading up
o the foundation of the Communities: Elisabeth Barker, *Britain In A Divided
Europe 1946–70* (Weidenfeld & Nicolson 1971); Walter Hallstein, *Europe in
the Making* (Allen and Unwin, 1972); Richard Mayne, *The Community of
Europe* (Gollancz 1962); Roger Morgan, *West European Politics since 1945,
the Shaping of the European Community* (Batsford, 1972); R.C. Mowat, *Creating the European Community* (Blandford, 1973). Stephen Holt, *Six European
States: the Countries of the European Community and their Political Systems*
Hamish Hamilton, 1970) provides necessary national background.

The following is a selection of works which I have found helpful on various aspects of the Communities. I have not repeated some of the titles already mentioned in footnotes.

British entry into Europe
Miriam Camps, *Britain and the European Community 1955–1963* (Oxford University Press, 1964); Philip Goodhart, *Full-hearted Consent; the Story of the Referendum Campaign* (Davis-Poynter, 1976); R.E.M. Irving, 'The UK Referendum June 1975', *European Law Review*, 1976; Uwe Kitzinger, *Diplomacy and Persuasion: How Britain Joined the Common Market* (Thames & Hudson, 1973).

Integration Theory
Ernst B. Haas *Beyond the Nation State* (Stanford University Press, 1964) Michael Hodges, *European Integration* (Penguin Books, 1972).

Institutions of the European Community

General: *The New Politics of European Integration*, edited by Ghita Ionescu (Macmillan, 1972), a collection of studies originally published in *Government and Opposition*, A. Shonfield, *Europe: Journey to an Unknown Destination* (Pelican, 1974); Ghita Ionescu, *Centripetal Politics: Governments and the New Centres of Power* (Hart-Davis, 1975); Michael Hodges (ed.), *European Integration* (Penguin, 1972); Christopher Tugendhat, *The Multinational* (Penguin, 1973).

Law: P.S.R.F. Mathijsen *A Guide to European Community Law* (Sweet and Maxwell/Matthew Bender, 1972); D. Lasok and J.W. Bridge, *Law and Institutions of the European Communities* (Butterworth 1973).

Institutions: *Working together: the Institutions of the European Community*, simply written guide by the Commission, European Economic Community Roger Broad and R.J. Jarrett, *Community Europe Today*, revised edn (Wolff, 1972); Donald Chapman, *The Road to European Union*, Sussex European Papers, Centre for Contemporary European Studies (University of Sussex, 1975); D. Coombes, *Politics and Bureaucracy in the European Community* (Allen and Unwin/PEP, 1970); Annette Morgan, *From Summit to Council: Evolution in the EEC* (Chatham House/PEP, 1976).

Parliament: *The European Parliament: Sovereignty and Direct Elections* Exploring European series (The Schools Unit, University of Sussex Centre for Contemporary European Studies, 1978); Chris Cook and Mary Francis, *The First European Elections: A Handbook and Guide* (Macmillan, 1979); John

Fitzmaurice, *The European Parliament* (Saxon House, 1979); David Marquand, *A Parliament for Europe* (Jonathan Cape, 1979).

Community and member states

Helen Wallace, William Wallace and Carole Webb (eds.), *Policy Making in
the European Communities* (Wiley, 1977); *The British People: their Voice in
Europe*, Hansard Society for Parliamentary Government (Saxon House, 1977)
on the consequences for entry on representative institutions; Helen Wallace,
National Governments and the European Communities (Chatham House/PEP,
1973); Michael Niblock, *The EEC: National Parliaments in Community
Decision-Making* (PEP European series 17, 1971); Margaret Stewart, *Trade
Unions in Europe* (Gower Economic Publications, 1974); Eirlys Roberts,
Consumers in the Common Market (European Studies 22, 1975); 'Transna-
tional Parties in the European Community', Geoffrey Pridham and Pippa
Pridham in *Political Parties in the European Community*, Policy Studies Insti-
tute, ed. Stanley Henig (Allen and Unwin, 1979); 'Social Policies in Europe',
The Economist Schools Brief, 8 April 1978; *Influencing Europe: A Guide for
Pressure Groups*, Roy Manley and Helen Hastings (Fabian Pamphlet 33,
1977).

Regional

A New Regional Policy for Europe, European Documentation EEC Brussels
1975/3; *Rural Depopulation*, Exploring Europe Autumn 1978, (The Schools
Unit, European Research Centre, University of Sussex); *The New Europe: An
Economic Geography of the EEC,* G.N. Minshull (Hodder and Stoughton,
1978).

Social

'Social Policies in Europe', *The Economist* Schools Brief, 8 April 1978;
Michael Shanks, *European Social Policy Today and Tomorrow* (Pergamon,
1977); Eirlys Roberts, *Consumers in the Common Market* (European Studies
22, 1975).

External Relations

Frans A.M. Alting von Geusau (ed.), *The External Relations of the European
Community* (Saxon House, 1974); Carol Ann Cosgrove and Kenneth J.
Twitchett (eds), *The New International Actors: The United Nations and the
European Economic Community* (Macmillan, 1970); P. Everts, *The European
Community in the World* (Rotterdam University Press, 1972); A.J. Galtung,
The European Community: A Super Power in the Making (Allen & Unwin,
1973); Roger Morgan, *High Politics/Low Politics* (Sage Publications, 1974);

William Wallace, 'Europe: The Changing International Context', *The World Today*, January 1975; *The European Community and the Developing Countries*, European Documentation 1977/1; *The Courier: Africa – Caribbean – Pacific – European Community*, published every two months by the Commission of the European Communities, 200, rue de la Loi, 1049 Brussels, Belgium.

Further Enlargement
Geoffrey Edwards and William Wallace, *A Wider European Community? Issues and Problems of Further Enlargement* (Federal Trust, 1976); Frank Ellis, *The European Community and the Third World*, European Studies nos. 19, 20 (EEC, 1974); *The Politics of Southern Europe*, European Studies 25 1976.

See also the numerous pamphlets published by the Community on other Community policies, for example, *The Common Agricultural Policy*, Commission of the European Communities 1977, *The Agricultural Policy of the European Community*, European Documentation 2/79, and *European Economic and Monetary Union*, European Documentation 1979.

Index

Note: The abbreviations of some European organisations are taken from the initials of their titles in French.

International Court of Justice, The Hague, 45

Irish Republic, Community membership, 32

Iron and Steel Workers Federation (FEDERAL), 85

Japan, trade relations with EEC, 125
Jenkins, Roy, 35, 55, 140, 149
Jones, Jack, 152

Kissinger, Henry, 11
Korean War, 10

Labour Party, British, and Europe, 5, 9, 29–30, 33, 35, 89
Law, Community, see Community Law
Living and Working Conditions, European Foundation for Improvement of, 110
lobbying of Community institutions, 85–6
Local Authorities, International Union of, 93
Lomé Conventions, 34, 74, 119–23
Luns Procedure, 74
'Luxembourg Compromise', 1966, 28–9, 55

Macmillan, Harold, 24, 25
Maghreb States and EEC, 126
management committees, 57
Mansholt Plan for agricultural reform, 146
Marchais, Georges, 90
Mashreq countries, agreements with EEC, 126
Mediterranean polices of EEC, 126
Merger Treaty, 1965, 28–9, 83
Messina Conference, 1955, 12
Mezzogiorno, 14, 22, 96
Mollet, Guy, 12
monetary compensatory amounts (MCAs), 144
Monetary Cooperation Fund, European (FECOM), 41, 140
Monetary System, European, (EMS), 140–2
Monnet, Jean, 3, 6–9, 12, 51, 151–2
Moro, Aldo, 12
Mouvement Républicain Populaire (MRP), 22, 89

Multifibre Agreements, 122
Municipalities, Council of European, 93

Nassau Conference 1962, 26
national sovereignty and Community membership, 35–7, 47
New Zealand agriculture, 32, 35
non-tariff barriers to trade, 17
Nordic Council, 33
North Atlantic Treaty Organisation (NATO), 10, 27, 125, 126–7
North Sea oil, 134
North-South Conference, 123, 134
Northern Ireland, 75, 100
Norway, rejects EEC membership, 31, 33, 131

OECD, (Organisation for Economic Cooperation and Development), 6, 25, 116
OEEC (Organisation for European Economic Cooperation), see OECD
oil crises, 1973, 1979, 133–5

Paisley, Rev. Ian, 67, 101
Paris, Treaty of, April 1951, 9
Permanent Representatives, Committee of, (COREPER), 29, 58, 60–1, 63, 79
Pleven, René, 12
political cooperation, 61–2
political groups in European Parliament, 67–8
political parties and EEC: British Labour Party, 89; Christian Democrat, 22, 67, 89, 91; Communist, 22, 67–8, 89–92; European Liberals and Democrats (ELD), 67, 91; Social Democrat, 89, 91; Socialist, 67, 90–1
Pompidou, Georges, 26, 30
Portugal and EEC membership, 129–31
Poverty Programme, EEC, 11
Powell, Enoch, 36, 103
professional qualifications, harmonisation, 18
Proudhon, P.J., 2

Randstad, 96
Referendum Campaign, British, 34–7
referendums, in Europe, 32, 33, 38
regional aids, 18, 96–8
Regional Development Fund, 71, 97–9